BOOK
OF
SHADOWS

About the Author

Migene González-Wippler (New York) is a self-initiated Witch, cultural anthropologist, and an author of more than twenty books. She lectures frequently and has worked for the American Institute of Physics, the American Museum of Natural History, and the United Nations in Vienna.

To Write to the Author

If you wish to contact the author or would like more information about this book, please write to the author in care of Llewellyn Worldwide and we will forward your request. Both the author and publisher appreciate hearing from you and learning of your enjoyment of this book and how it has helped you. Llewellyn Worldwide cannot guarantee that every letter written to the author can be answered, but all will be forwarded. Please write to:

Migene González-Wippler
⅘ Llewellyn Worldwide
2143 Wooddale Drive, Dept. 978-0-7387-0213-1
Woodbury, Minnesota 55125-2989, U.S.A.
Please enclose a self-addressed stamped envelope for reply,
or $1.00 to cover costs. If outside U.S.A., enclose
international postal reply coupon.

Many of Llewellyn's authors have websites with additional information and resources. For more information, please visit our website at http://www.llewellyn.com.

BOOK
OF
SHADOWS

MIGENE
GONZÁLEZ-WIPPLER

Llewellyn Publications
Woodbury, Minnesota

First Edition
Fourth Printing, 2008

Book design by Alexander Negrete
Cover design by Llewellyn Art Department
Interior illustrations by Llewellyn Art Department
Translated by Migene González-Wippler

Llewellyn is a registered trademark of Llewellyn Worldwide, Ltd.

Library of Congress Cataloging-in-Publication Data
Gonzalez-Wippler, Migene.
  [Libro de las sombras. English]
  Book of shadows / Migene Gonzalez-Wippler.— 1st ed.
      p.   cm.
  Includes bibliographical references.
  ISBN 13: 978-0-7387-0213-1
  ISBN 10: 0-7387-0213-7 (alk. paper)
   1. Witchcraft. I. Title.

BF 1566.G6613 2005
133.4'3—dc22   2005044997

Llewellyn Worldwide does not participate in, endorse, or have any authority or responsibility concerning private business transactions between our authors and the public.

All mail addressed to the author is forwarded but the publisher cannot, unless specifically instructed by the author, give out an address or phone number.

Any Internet references contained in this work are current at publication time, but the publisher cannot guarantee that a specific location will continue to be maintained. Please refer to the publisher's website for links to authors' websites and other sources.

The publisher and the author assume no liability for any injuries caused to the reader that may result from the reader's use of the content contained herein. Some herbs described in this work are dangerous. Use common sense and caution when contemplating the practices described in the work.

Llewellyn Publications
A Division of Llewellyn Worldwide, Ltd.
2143 Wooddale Drive, Dept. 978-0-7387-0213-1
Woodbury, Minnesota 55125-2989, U.S.A.
www.llewellyn.com

Printed in the United States of America

Other Books by Migene González-Wippler

Amuletos y Talismanes

Angelorum: El libro de los ángeles

Cabala para el mundo moderno

The Complete Book of Amulets & Talismans

The Complete Book of Spells, Ceremonies & Magic

Dreams and What They Mean to You

El libro completo de magia, hechizos, y ceremonias

El libro de las sombras

Keys to the Kingdom: Jesus & the Mystic Kabbalah

La magia de las piedras y los cristales

La magia y tú

Las llaves del reino: Jesús y la cábala cristiana

Luna, Luna: Magia, poder y seducción

Peregrinaje: la vida después de la muerte

Santería: La Religión

Santería: mis experiencias en la Religión

Santeria: the Religion: Faith, Rites, Magic

Sueños: Lo que significan para usted

*What Happens After Death:
Scientific & Personal Evidence for Survival*

Kabbalah for the Modern World

This book is dedicated to Gerald Gardner, Doreen Valiente,
Alex Sanders, Sybil Leek, Herman Slater,
Scott Cunningham, Valerie Worth

And all those who sleep in the Goddess' embrace

An' it harm none, do as thou wilt
(Wiccan Rede)

CONTENTS

INTRODUCTION

Most of my readers will be surprised to see a book on Wicca written by me. I am generally associated with books on Ceremonial Magic, Kabbalah, Santeria, dreams, angels, and life after death. They will be doubly surprised to learn that Wicca was one of my first loves and that long before I became involved in my research on Santeria and my Kabbalah work I had already undergone a self-initiation into the mysteries of Witchcraft, and I continue to this day to observe its practices and beliefs. This happened about thirty years ago when very few good books were available on the practical aspects of the Craft. Among these early books were those written by Gerald Gardner, Doreen Valiente, Ray Buckland, Lady Sheba, Sybil Leek, Herman Slater, Yvonne and Gavin Frost, and Stewart Farrar. There were other books written at the time purporting to be written by Witches but one single glance through their pages would immediately let you know that their authors knew very little about the rituals and practices of Witchcraft. I was living in Vienna during this period as I was under contract as an Associate English

Editor for the United Nations Industrial Development Organization (UNIDO). I had read in a magazine an interview with Alex Sanders, who was known in England as the King of the Witches, and I decided to travel to London to meet him. I contacted the editors at the magazine and told them I also wanted to interview Alex and they very generously gave me his address and telephone number. I called him from Vienna and he immediately agreed to meet with me. During this time I was just flirting with the idea of joining a coven and being initiated into the Craft. I knew very little about the initiations and rites of Wicca.

Alex, his wife Maxine, and their daughter Maya lived in a London flat, below street level. One entered the place from the street, going down a short flight of stairs that led to the front door. I arrived at the flat around 3 PM. Alex was holding court in a small, shadowy drawing room, surrounded by several of his Witches. He was a short, thin man, with slightly hunched shoulders and thinning, dark hair. His expression was open and amiable and he had a winning smile. He greeted me graciously and introduced me to Maxine, who acted as his High Priestess, and to the other members of the coven. We sat together on a much worn settee, covered with several throws embossed with Celtic designs. He immediately produced his Book of Shadows, a large tome with black covers, where all the rites, initiations, spells and other secrets of the Craft had been painstakingly handwritten. Many of the pages were worn at the edges and the writing was rather faded.

He explained that he received his first initiation from his grandmother and that all his Witches had to copy the book, word by word, drawing by drawing, and spell by spell to the last page, after they had been initiated into his coven. He was charming and full of information and ended by inviting me to join him and the coven that evening during one of their regular meetings. But first we were to go to the coven's usual "hangout," a pub near Alex's house for a quick meal. As I go into some detail on what happened at the pub that night elsewhere in this book, I will not mention it here.

We returned to the flat around 10 PM. There were between eight and ten people present, all of them initiated Witches. As soon as we arrived, they began the preparations for the ceremony. There were three or four women besides Maxine, and an equal number of men. I knew Witches in Alex's coven conducted their rites "skyclad," that is, naked, and I had no problem with that, as long as I was not asked to disrobe as well. Alex assured me that was not necessary. I was to stand outside the circle and watch what went on. Everything proceeded without any problems. The men went inside one of the rooms and took off their clothes, and returned to the place where the rite was to take place. Maxine was wearing a white, see-through, floor-length gown; Alex was naked and so were the other women. But then, something very alarming took place. From one of the cupboards lining the walls, Alex took out a long rope and several black-handled knives that he distributed among the Witches. I also saw what looked like a silken whip and a large sword. I was suddenly petrified with fear. The most terrifying thoughts began to course through my mind. After all, I did not know these people. As charming and gentle as Alex seemed, I did not know him either. I had visions of my dead body floating down the Thames after being savagely attacked by the Witches with all those terrible knives. With shaking legs, I approached Alex and told him that I did not think that I could remain for the ceremony. I was not sure if he would let me go. Maybe he and the other men would jump at me and hold me hostage. But he smiled gently and nodded his head, and said that it was all right, he understood. The rest of the coven watched me in silence as I gathered my belongings and escaped into the night. I can only imagine what they must have said after I left. But I knew nothing about the rites of Wicca. I did not know that the "terrible" black-handled knives were athames, an intrinsic part of the Wicca ceremony. I did not know that the whip, the cord, and the sword were all necessary and quite harmless implements of the Craft. I did not know because Wicca had been so long shrouded in mystery, so long persecuted by ignorance and superstition, that its most sacred and pure rites were deemed dangerous and obscene. Not knowing these things deprived me of what would have been undoubtedly one of the great religious experiences of my lifetime. That will forever remain one of the deepest regrets of my life.

Upon returning to New York I discovered a bookstore that was reputed to be a Witches' gathering place. It was located in Brooklyn and its name was The Warlock Shoppe. Later it was moved to Manhattan under a new name, The Magickal Childe. The owner and manager was Herman Slater, who was to become a close friend. Herman had written two books. One was titled *A Book of Pagan Rituals*, the other, *A Magical Formulary*. These books are still available and are required reading for anyone seriously interested in the history and practices of the Craft. A third book, *Introduction to Witchcraft*, is now out of print and hard to find. The first two books eventually became classics in the neopagan movement. I first visited Herman's store in Brooklyn and followed it when it moved to Manhattan. Through the years I became very close to Herman and we developed a rare friendship. Herman was not an easy person to approach and he seemed distant and changeable at times, but he was immensely knowledgeable and very willing to share his knowledge with those who were sincere in their quest. It was through his prodding that I eventually underwent the self-initiation of Wicca. When he died in the mid nineties, I truly mourned his passing. It is very sad to find that today Herman's books and his work are set aside by the younger pagan generation and classified as unimportant and passé. It is easy now to write about Wicca. It has become an "in" phenomenon. It was not so during the Vietnam era when Herman Slater, Alex Sanders, and Ray Buckland conducted their rites and wrote or spoke about the ancient mysteries. The works of Sybil Leek, Lady Sheba, and Stewart Farrar added luster to the radiance. We all must be grateful for their efforts and their teachings. They were true pioneers, following closely on the footsteps of Gerald Gardner and Doreen Valiente. Later on, Margot Adler wrote *Drawing Down the Moon*, Laurie Cabot opened the gates of Salem, and that completed the magic circle. Wicca was on. Many different pagan systems followed; the Craft evolved and grew in multiple ways. It became rich with a new, all-encompassing vision. New, bright minds added to the renewed splendor. Scott Cunningham, the Campanellis, and many others all helped add to the Wicca renaissance.

Today Wicca has many branches and denominations such as the Gardnerian, Seax, Alexandrian, Norse, Druidic, Celtic, and many others. This book was written from the Gardnerian viewpoint. It follows the classical Wicca tradition and many Witches will not agree with some of the practices I mention in the book as they will differ from their own. That is part of the richness of Wicca, its willingness to evolve and diversify. The book was written originally in Spanish and translated into English. I decided to write the book because the Craft has been growing rapidly in Latin America. Many Hispanics are attracted to it because they share its Celtic background through their Spanish heritage. They also find a kinship between its love of nature and natural forces and those of some Latin American practices, such as Santeria.

The Book of Shadows is the name given to the "diary" of a Witch, but in reality it is more than a diary; it is a compendium of all the practices, beliefs, rituals, and spells of Witchcraft. The word "Witchcraft" (*brujeria*) has always been associated with the practice of magic in Latin America, but in Spain, where the Craft has been assiduously practiced since the Middle Ages, Witchcraft is recognized as a religion based on the beliefs and magical practices of the ancient Celts. The great Spanish master Francisco Goya y Lucientes captured many of the practices of the Celtic "brujeria" in the black and white drawings that were later to be known as "Caprichos" (whims). The Spanish Inquisition, the most ferocious and machiavellian in all of Europe, persecuted and killed thousands of innocent people accused of practicing Witchcraft in Spain. Goya himself was suspected of sympathizing and maybe even practicing Witchcraft and only his powerful contacts with King Charles IV saved him from indictment by the courts of the Spanish Inquisition.

The Celts were a group of nomadic tribes who extended their influence all over Europe, including England, France,

Germany and Spain between the fifth and first centuries B.C. Their religion was based on the worship of deities identified with the forces of nature. Their priests were known as druids. They spread all over Spain around 1 B.C. and their influence was so powerful that it was able to survive the Moorish and Visigoth conquests.

Spain was greatly influenced by the magico-religious beliefs of the Celts and the Inquisition persecuted these practices from 1478 to 1834. The inquisitors were chosen by the Pope and most of them were Dominican monks. The most cruel of the Spanish inquisitors was also a Dominican monk named Tomas de Torquemada, who was the confessor and spiritual counselor of the Spanish monarchs, Ferdinand and Isabella. It was Ferdinand and Isabella who instituted the Spanish Inquisition. The cruel practices of the Inquisition were eventually brought to the Americas, notably Mexico and Peru, where thousands of innocent people were executed as heretics and sorcerers.

The papal name of the Inquisition was the "Roman Inquisition and the Holy Office." The Holy Office lasted until 1965, when Pope Paul VI, forced by the many complaints received, changed its name to the "Congregation for the Doctrine of the Faith." So powerful was the influence of the Inquisition in Europe that the practice of Witchcraft was forbidden in England until 1951, more than a century after the "Holy Office" closed its bloodied doors.

In Europe, the practice of Witchcraft extended to Italy, where Witches are known as "stregas." Aradia, one of the most popular names of the Goddess, can be traced to the Wicca tradition in Italy.

In 1954, an Englishman named Gerald Gardner published a book titled *Witchcraft Today* where he claimed to have been initiated into the practices of the "Old Religion" by a coven of Witches. Although many people today doubt Gardner's claims, his book was very helpful in revealing many of the practices and beliefs of Wicca. As a result many covens were organized throughout England. One of the most famous covens based on Gardner's teachings was the one created by Alex Sanders, who was to be known eventually as England's king of the Witches. His teachings are now known as the Alexandrian tradition. Many of the covens that exist throughout the world today are based on Gardner's or Sanders' teachings. But there are many other traditions that are also popular, like Ray Buckland's Seax, the Celtic, Saxon, Druidic, Huna, Algard, and Sicilian traditions. The Wicca practices presented in this book follow the Gardnerian/Alexandrian traditions.

The beliefs and practices of Wicca became especially popular in the United States during the 1960s. The identification of natural forces with supernatural entities, the beneficial practices of Witchcraft, the poetic beauty of its rituals, the intrinsic power of its magic and its respect towards life, human equality, and nature's creatures all found an echo in the American spirit, which had been badly bruised by the futile Vietnam war and was in great need of Wicca's spirituality. This popularity has grown through the years and today there are thousands of covens in the United States, some of which advertise freely on the Internet, in magazines, and in other media.

In the beginning, many people saw Wicca as a covert adoration of malignant forces, associating the Witches with Satanism.

The fact that the god of Wicca, known by many as Karnayna, wears a crown of deer horns helped foster the erroneous view that Witches worshipped the devil. But in reality Karnayna is a woodlands deity and its horned crown represents the hunt. Witches do not worship Satan, but the forces of nature. They see their religion as part of ancient pagan practices that pre-dated both Christianity and Satanism. That is why Wicca is known as the "Old Religion," whose practices date from the times of the Celts, more than 2,500 years ago.

Wicca is based on an initiation system that is carried out by each individual coven. The covens are usually headed by a priest and priestess who represent the god and the goddess worshipped by the Witches. This is not true of all covens, as there are also all male and all female groups as well as groups that function with either a priest or a priestess.

The god and goddess of Wicca have many names and the names vary from coven to coven. Among these names are Karnayna (Cernunnos) and Aradia for the god and goddess respectively, and these are the names we will use in this book. The deities are mythological figures.

In Tuscan lore, Aradia was the daughter of the goddess Diana and lived in the heavens most of her life. Her mother sent her to earth to teach the arts of magic to all Witches. When her mission was over she returned to heaven but is always ready to grant the desires of Witches. Among the many powers she can grant are the abilities to communicate with the dead, heal the sick and predict the future. Charles Leland, in his book *Aradia: The Gospel of the Witches*, writes that when a Witch wishes to ask a favor or "boon" from Aradia, she must go to an open field at midnight carrying with her food, wine, a talisman, and a small, red bag filled with salt. She then blesses herself with the wine and water and pledges her allegiance to the goddess. In Wicca, Aradia is seen as a lunar deity like her mother Diana.

Karnayna, or Cernunnos, is a Celtic deity who rules over fertility, life, animals, and the underworld. He is known as the "Horned One." According to tradition, Karnayna sometimes carries a purse filled with coins. He is usually depicted with deer antlers and represents the woods and the fauna. Very often he is depicted sitting down with crossed legs. He is said to be born at the winter solstice, marries the goddess at Beltane, and dies at the summer solstice to be reborn again in winter. He alternates with the Moon Goddess in ruling over life and death, repeating the cycle of death and rebirth.

Of these two deities, the most important in Gardnerian Witchcraft is Aradia, also known as the White Goddess or the Great Goddess, who is identified with the moon, nature, and the Cosmic Mother. For this reason, in Gardnerian/Alexandrian covens, the High Priestess, who represents Aradia, is the one who leads the coven and establishes its rules and requisites.

PART ONE

WICCA

THE WITCHES' COVEN

Witches usually work within groups known as covens, although there are solitary practitioners of the religion who prefer to observe the rituals and festivals without the help of others. People who are uninitiated are known as "cowans." Solitary practitioners initiate themselves into the mysteries of the religion. The number of people in a coven vary from group to group. The traditional number of Witches in a coven is supposed to be thirteen, but there are covens composed of more or less than that number.

The coven exists to worship the forces of nature, especially the god and goddess, and to help each other in peace and harmony. Within the coven the Witches form a sacred bond rooted in ancient traditions and powerful oaths.

The principal foundation of the coven's power is the Witches' pyramid. This pyramid is spiritual in nature. One side represents the dynamic and controlled will of the Witches; the second side represents the power of imagination through which the Witches visualize their wishes clearly so that they may be realized; the third is the Witches' total and absolute faith in their ability to achieve their desires through the power of magic; and the fourth represents silence, as the Witches must never reveal who they are or the powers they possess. In other words, the four sides of the pyramid are will, imagination, faith, and silence. These are the basic rules of Wicca. Through the power of this pyramid the Witches accumulate a profound knowledge of natural laws and of the motion of the cosmic tides. The origin of the power of these tides is the movement of the sun, the moon, and the planets, including the earth itself.

Witches believe that it is not enough to acquire knowledge and power. It is also necessary to know how to focus and direct that knowledge and power towards that which is desired. The aims of any magical work must never include doing harm to other people or things or gathering power to dominate others.

Many covens meet once a week, although there may be special occasions when the High Priestess convokes a meeting during an emergency.

Others meet only once a month during the full moon. Some meet also during the new moon. These meetings are known as Esbats. The minimum amount of Esbats that must be held by a coven is thirteen, the number of full moons in a year. There are also eight annual festivals known as Sabbats, which include the solstices and the equinoxes. In the next chapter we will discuss the Sabbats in detail and the rituals that are celebrated at those times.

During their meetings the Witches cast a Circle within which they conduct their ceremonies. Once the magical work is started, the Circle must never be broken. The traditional size of the Circle is nine feet in diameter, but this is seldom observed by most Witches mostly because it is too small to accommodate everyone in the group comfortably. The rule of thumb is for the members of the coven to form a circle by holding hands with arms extended. The space formed in this manner then becomes the Circle's perimeter. There are two movements made within the Circle. The movement to the right is known as deosil; to the left, is widdershins. The purpose of the ceremony decides the direction in which the coven will move, but for White Magic purposes, the movement is always deosil. Widdershins is usually associated with negative magic, but it can also be used for positive purposes. The Circle is cast from east to east with the magic sword, usually by the High Priestess, although any member of the coven may cast it if necessary. The movement is always deosil. The Circle is usually painted on the floor with white chalk, although some covens that have a permanent temple paint the circle in white paint. Four white candles are placed on the floor in the four cardinal points within the Circle's perimeter. The High Priestess walks around the Circle with the sword, pointing to the floor with the sword's tip to consecrate the Circle, east to east. Witches always enter the Circle from the east, as it represents sunrise and White Magic.

Most Witches place their altar in the center of the Circle. It usually holds one or two white candles, an incense burner, a dish for salt and another for water, a wine goblet, the ritual sword, and sometimes the images of the god and goddess.

The Gardnerian altar also holds a scourge and ritual cords. Of course, this varies from coven to coven.

Covens usually meet at the same place. This place is known as the Covenstead. In ancient times the area where the Witches lived outside their Covenstead was known as the Covendom and it extended for approximately three miles (one league). Different Covendoms were not supposed to overlap each other as each coven claimed the Covendom's area as their own. In modern times, where Witches may live many miles away from their Covenstead, the concept of the Covendom is seldom observed. But modern Witches still refer to their place of meeting as the Covenstead. The coven members usually greet each other with a hug and a kiss and the words, "Blessed Be" or "Merry Meet." When they separate, they embrace again and say, "Merry Part" or "Merry Meet Again."

The main purpose of each ceremony is to raise the Cone of Power. Without the Cone the ceremony is incomplete and the power of the Witches cannot be concentrated. To raise the Cone, the Witches hold hands and begin to move quickly around the Circle, always deosil, until they are running. As they move they chant the Witches' runes that are the heart of Wicca. We will discuss the runes in detail in chapter 5. The runes contain an invocation to the god and goddess, asking them to descend to the Circle and grant the coven's wishes.

Many people with astral vision claim to have seen the Cone of Power rising in the middle of the Circle like a pillar of radiant energy. When the High Priestess, who usually leads the raising of the Cone, judges that sufficient power has been accumulated, she asks the Witches to stop. At that moment, this energy is directed by the coven through concentrated will and meditation towards the goal that they intend to achieve. The decision on how to use the Cone's power is always made before the start of the ceremony. It is generally directed to accomplish the needs of one of the members of the coven, and it is always used to accomplish one thing only. This is based on one of the best known laws of magic, which says that energy directed towards more than one goal is lost and dissipated. Witches alternate the use of the Cone of Power among themselves quite harmoniously. And because each member will receive the Cone's energy during one of the meetings, they are very willing to help each other, sharing their combined energies like good brethren.

The Cone of Power can be used for healing purposes, and to solve love and money problems and any other personal crises one of the coven members may be facing. The Cone's energy depends on the concentration and mental power of the Witches and it can achieve miraculous things when it is properly raised and directed. This is one of the reasons the Witches work together so harmoniously. It is simply easier to achieve a goal through the accumulated energies of many persons than with the energies of just one.

The Cone is closely linked with the Witches' pyramid because without will, imagination, faith, and silence very little can be accomplished. The other important element is the Circle.

Witches believe that the Circle helps to concentrate the Cone's energy and holds it in place so that it will not dissipate quickly. For this reason, the first action undertaken by the High Priestess or whoever is directing the ceremony is to cast the Circle with the help of the magic sword or the magic dagger known as the athame. Once the Circle is cast the Witches must not leave it except with great care. To leave the Circle once it is cast, the person makes two cuts on the imaginary Circle with the athame, one on his right and one on his left, opening an invisible gate. This is done on the east of the Circle. He can then then leave through that astral doorway. When he returns he must enter on the same side and seal the gate by crisscrossing the athame's blade over the Circle's perimeter three times in a swinging motion.

Sometimes, when the Witches want to contact a person who is not present, they may use the Cone's power to create an "elemental." This is a mental projection that takes the form of a ball of energy or a bird. The elemental is sent to the individual with special instructions that it should return to the coven or the Witch who created it with the information required.

Witches believe that magic is nothing more than the ability to manipulate the forces of nature to acquire what is desired. To them, cosmic energy is neutral. It is the person who uses it who makes it good or bad.

To ensure that they are not using this power in a negative way, Witches adhere to one essential creed or rede. It says simply, "An you harm none, do as you will." This means that the Witch is free to use the cosmic powers for anything he or she may want provided no one is hurt in the process. Whenever this basic rule is broken, the magic being practiced is black.

Another important law followed by Witches is the Law of Three. This law says that any act carried out by an individual will return to that person with triple force, be it for good or for evil. No one is exempt from this law, not even organizations, and that is the reason why Witches are careful not to commit negative acts against anyone or anything, as they know such actions will be result in very negative backlash against them. When someone does something particularly disagreeable to them, Witches can invoke the Law of Three against that person or persons and then wait for results. A friend of mine, who is a third-degree Witch, told me this story. She was a student at New York University when these events happened. She had been unable to pay her gas bill for two months because she had been taking care of her mother who was recuperating from a stroke. As a result her financial situation was very difficult. She went to the offices of the gas company that serviced her house and asked for an extension. The officer in charge was completely unsympathetic and told her that not only was she not going to get an extension, but that she also had to add $300 more to her bill as a deposit. My friend said nothing. She simply turned her back on the man and called on the Law of Three against the gas company. Within twenty-four hours, the company's computer block that included her residence malfunctioned, erasing all the accounts that it contained. Thousands of people had free gas for weeks and the company lost millions of dollars as a result. Since the company had to start the accounts anew, my friend's outstanding bill did not have to be paid. This is only one of the many stories I have heard about the awesome powers of the Law of Three. Incidentally, you do not have to be a Witch to invoke the Law of Three. It works for anyone, provided the individual that invokes it adheres to its strict principles.

There are other magic laws observed in Wicca. Among them is the Law of Contact, according to which things that have been in contact with a person maintain the contact long after they have been separated from that person. For that reason, Witches believe that personal objects may be used to influence a person through magical means. Handkerchiefs, socks, combs, articles of clothing, letters, all may be used in magic spells with very real results. The principle behind the magic is that whatever happens to the object will also happen to the person.

Another important law is the Law of Similarity, also known as imitative magic. According to this law certain acts will result in similar acts. This is done in symbolic form. For example, a very simple love spell to unite a man and a woman is cast by inscribing the names of the two persons on the back of two red image candles, one in the shape of a man and the other in the shape of a woman. The two candles are rubbed with cinnamon or rose oil and tied together with a red ribbon. They are then lit and allowed to burn out with the firm wish that likewise the two people will burn with love for each other. Some Witches would consider this a Black Magic spell as it is interfering with free will, but black or white, this is a very popular and effective love spell that uses the Law of Similarity. If you wish to cast this spell and have difficulty locating image candles, you can use ordinary wax to form the images.

Witches also believe in another type of elemental that has an autonomous existence. These are known as elemental forces and include gnomes, undines, sylphs or fairies, and salamanders. They are known as elemental forces because they are associated with the four elements. The gnomes are the regents of the Earth element and are visualized as tiny bearded man-like creatures. They are believed to live in the center of the earth and own all mines, metals, precious stones and minerals. The undines rule Water and have the appearance of beautiful maidens made of a translucent blue vapor. The live in rivers and lakes and own all that pertains to the water realm. The sylphs or fairies rule Air and are visualized as lovely minute creatures with gossamer wings. They control all that belongs to the Air element. Salamanders rule Fire and may materialize as tiny dragons made of fire. They may be seen dancing among the flames of a bright fire by those with astral vision. Fairies are particularly favored by Witches. The king and queen of the fairies were immortalized by Shakespeare in *A Midsummer Night's Dream*. He named them Titania and Oberon, or maybe they revealed their names to him. Many Witches make offers to the fairies on the eve of the summer solstice, also known as Midsummer Night.

Witches choose their magical names as soon as they enter a coven. Most Witches use names associated with the Goddess, nature, or a quality they admire. Some typical Witches' names are White Eagle, Silverstream, Moonbeam, Serenity, Diana, Selene, Seawolf, and Mariluna.

According to Wicca, the Goddess has three manifestations that are reflected in all women: the Maiden, the Mother, and the Crone. All women go through these three phases. The Maiden is a young woman, not necessarily a virgin; the Mother is a woman in the full bloom of her femininity; and the Crone is an older woman, who has acquired great wisdom with her years. Of the three, the Crone is the most respected of the Goddess' manifestations. Often, when the High Priestess reaches the Crone's phase she may decide to leave the coven to allow a younger Witch to take her place. In most instances, the other Witches insist that she remain, especially if she is a High Priestess of great power. If she still decides to leave, she is allowed to do so and the coven gives her one year and a day to change her mind. Should she decide to return after this time, the new High Priestess must step aside and let the senior one resume her place.

Before they agree to accept a newcomer into their Circle, the members of the coven study the person's circumstances carefully to ensure he or she will be a trustworthy addition to the group. Only when they are fully convinced that the aspirant fulfills all the necessary requirements is the person admitted to the coven. Once admitted, the person is invited to attend the next Esbat or Sabbath where he or she will receive the First Degree initiation.

There are three levels of initiations in Wicca: First, Second, and Third Degrees. When a Witch receives the Third Degree initiation he is judged to have enough knowledge and experience in the Craft to start his own coven.

Not all Witches abandon their Covenstead when they receive the Third Degree initiation, but those who do receive the blessing of the High Priest and High Priestess. Each new coven is considered a branch of the old Covenstead. In Gardnerian and Alexandrian covens, the High Priestess wears a green garter on her left thigh. Each time one of the members of her group starts a new coven, the High Priestess places a silver buckle on her garter. There are old covens where the High Priestess sports a garter filled with many silver buckles, each one a symbol of a new coven born of her own.

All Covensteads have a name that is usually chosen by the High Priestess or the members of the group. Among common names for a coven are: The Circle of Aradia, The Moon's Circle, The Moon's Children, and The Silver Star.

Witches zealously guard the secrets and rules of their coven and protect each other. A Witch who betrays his coven or one of its members is immediately cast out of the Circle and often cursed by the High Priestess, the High Priest, and the entire coven. One of the most common curses is: "May the curse of the Great Goddess be upon him, may he never be born again on this earth, and may he remain forever in the Christian hell."

The idea that Witches fly on broomsticks dates from the Middle Ages. Farmers believed that crops would grow higher if they jumped through the fields on a broom. The flying ointment, made of hallucinogenic substances, was also used by Witches of the period. It was rubbed over the body producing a feeling of euphoria and out-of-the body experiences. Many Witches used it during their rituals, thus giving rise to the legend that Witches could fly. This practice was abandoned eventually, especially when it was discovered that hallucinogens can cause great damage to the nervous system.

Another important rule of Wicca is that Witches cannot accept money in exchange for their magical help. The members of a coven are not supposed to argue among themselves. Any dispute among the Witches is usually settled by the High Priestess or a council of elders.

In some covens, when a Witch commits an offense against the group and repents, he confesses his fault on his bent knees at the feet of the High Priestess. She then passes a sentence with the coven's approval. Usually these offenses are punished with a few lashes from her whip, which is made of silken braids and causes no harm. The Witch then kisses the High Priestess' hand as well as the whip, in thanks for the punishment which implies the coven's forgiveness. The Witches all embrace their repentant brother or sister and celebrate the reconciliation with the usual cakes and wine.

The High Priestess is given the title of Lady by the members of her coven. She may be Lady Silverstone, Lady Moonbeam, or Lady Owen. This is especially the case with the Gardnerian and Alexandrian covens. The High Priest, on the other hand, is never or seldom addressed as Lord. The High Priestess usually has a helper known as the Maiden who aids her during the rituals.

In modern times, Wicca has added new magical elements to its practices. A divination, which in ancient times was confined to tea leaves, tarot cards, and crystal balls, now include elements of astrology, Kabbalah, and Ceremonial Magic. This emphasizes the fact that Wicca is a dynamic, evolving religion whose members have assimilated new magical concepts without abandoning their traditional beliefs and practices.

2

Festivals, Sabbaths, and Esbats

A s I explained in the preceding chapter, Gardnerian Witchcraft celebrates two types of ceremonies. The most common takes place during the reunions known as Esbats, once a week and generally on Saturdays. Sabbaths are conducted during the eight annual festivals and during the full moon. Some covens who meet once a month, during the full moon, consider this monthly meeting an Esbat. Sometimes several covens get together to celebrate one of the eight annual festivals.

The annual festivals are closely connected with nature's cycles, agriculture, and animal husbandry, all of which were of great importance in ancient times when the practice of Wicca was part of farming.

The astronomical cycles that mark the beginning of the stations are also part of Wiccan celebrations, but they were not as important in ancient times.

The eight festivals are divided into two classes. The four most important are celebrated on February 2 (Candlemas), April 30 (Beltane), August 1 (Lammas), and October 31 (Samhain, also known as Hallowmass and Halloween). The four lesser festivals are celebrated at the start of the four seasons: March 21 (spring equinox), June 21 (summer solstice), September 21 (autumn equinox), and December 21 (winter solstice).

The eight festivals are known as the Wheel of Life because they mark periods of great importance for the earth and for humanity.

February 2—Candlemas

This festival observes the ancient Roman rites known as the Lupercalia, in honor of the god Pan. Romans believed this day to be of great fertility and the priests of Pan roamed the streets with long strips of wolves' skins with which they flogged all the women they found in their paths. This was believed to make the women more fertile and help them conceive many children.

In some covens, the High Priestess guides her group in traditional dances until they reach the place where the Candlemas ceremony is to take place. One of these dances is known as the Volta, where the Witches dance in pairs. This dance originated in Italy where Witchcraft was very popular in ancient times.

The High Priestess forms the Magic Circle with the black-handled knife known as the athame. The High Priest joins inside the circle with his sword in the right hand and the athame in the left. The magic weapons are placed upon the altar and the High Priest then proceeds to give the Five-Fold Kiss to the High Priestess.

The First Kiss is given by the High Priest on the feet of the High Priestess; the Second Kiss on her knees; the Third Kiss on her lower abdomen; the Fourth Kiss on her breasts, and the Fifth Kiss on her lips. Each time he kisses her, he blesses the area with certain ritualistic words we will discuss later on when we present the High Ceremony of Wicca. From these words comes the traditional greeting of Wicca: "Blessed Be."

After she has received the Five-Fold Kiss, the High Priestess says Blessed Be and gives the Five-Fold Kiss to the High Priest. She then recites the following invocation:

> *Dreaded Lord of Death and Resurrection,*
> *Of Life and Giver of Life,*
> *Our god, whose name is Mystery of Mysteries,*
> *Grant strength to our hearts,*
> *Permit that light crystallizes in our blood,*
> *Giving us the gift of resurrection.*
> *There is nothing in us that does not come from the gods.*
> *Descend, we beseech thee, upon your servant and priest.*

This is a call to the god Karnayna to descend and take possession of the High Priest. After the invocation the ceremony begins. If there are initiations planned for this day, they take place now. Some covens celebrate the Great Rite, which we will discuss later on.

After the ritual comes to an end, the Witches dance, exchange pleasantries, and eat the special offers of the festival, which always include sweet wine and cakes. Sometimes they play special games, such as the Candle Game during which the male Witches sit in a circle and proceed to pass a lit candle among themselves. The female Witches stand behind them and try to blow out the candle. When one of the female Witches blows out the candle, the male Witch who held it loses the game. He must then face the female Witch who gives three light lashings with her ritual whip, which is known as the scourge. The male Witch must then give the Five-Fold Kiss to the female Witch. The candle is lit again and the game continues. This is one of the many games Witches play during the Sabbaths.

March 21—Spring Equinox

This ritual often uses a wheel as a symbol of the Wheel of Life. Some Witches use a round mirror and others place four pieces of wood on the altar crossed over each other to form eight points. The eight points are held together by a strip of leather or metal and symbolize the eight festivals and the Wheel of Life. A white candle is placed on each side of the symbol.

The High Priestess proceeds to cast the Magic Circle within which is placed a large cauldron filled with flammable ingredients. The High Priestess stands on the west of the circle facing the High Priest who stands on the east. Each hold their athames in their right hands. The High Priestess recites the following invocation:

We light this fire today,
In the presence of the Holy Ones,
Without malice, without jealousy, and without envy,
Without fear of anything that exists under the light of the Sun,
Except the great gods.
We invoke you, O Light of Life,
Be thou a brilliant flame before us,
Be thou a radiant star above us,
Be thou a path without obstacles beneath us.
Kindle thou within our hearts
A flame of love towards our neighbors,
Towards our enemies, our friends, our loved ones,
And towards every human being who resides upon Earth.
O merciful son of Cerridwen, may love vibrate in our hearts
from the lowest creature that exists on the world
to the Highest Name of all.

The High Priestess traces a pentagram or five-pointed star in the air with her wand, which she then gives to the High Priest with her scourge. (The pentagram is a new addition to the rites of Wicca and originates in the rituals of Ceremonial Magic based on the Kabbalah.)

The Maiden, who is the assistant to the High Priestess, lights a candle and gives it to the High Priest. He uses the candle to set fire to the ingredients within the cauldron. He then takes the High Priestess' hand and they both jump over the flames inside the cauldron. The other Witches, in pairs, also jump over the cauldron.

This is a ritual of purification and Witches believe that jumping over the fire purifies them from negative vibrations.

After the rite the Witches proceed to play games, dance, drink wine and eat fruits and cake. Some covens conduct this festival in the open to avoid the dangers of fire but others prefer the privacy of the coven's meeting place.

During this festival the area surrounding the circle is adorned with flowers and some covens choose one of the youngest Witches as the Queen of Spring. This Witch receives all the flowers that surrounded the circle after the rite is over.

May 1—Beltane

This is the oldest of Wicca's festivals and the one which has survived nearly intact. Among the ancient Druids it was a festival of fire known as Beltane, a name still used by most Witches. In Germany the festival is known as Walpurgisnacht in honor of a saint of the eighth century.

In Roman times, April 30—Beltane's eve—was observed as Pluto's festival. Pluto was the Roman god of the Dead and the Underworld. Roman mythology borrowed the following legend from the Greeks but changed the names of the gods.

Pluto ruled the impenetrable darkness of Tartarus, where human souls go after death. This desolate region was believed to exist in the depths of the earth. One day, as Pluto roamed the earth in search of his enemies, he was seen by Venus, the goddess of love, who was playing with her small son Cupid. Venus told Cupid to send one of his arrows into Pluto's heart so that he would fall in love with the first woman who came across his path. Cupid obeyed his mother and shot one of his arrows into the heart of the indomitable god of the Underworld. At that moment, Proserpine, the only daughter of

Ceres, the goddess of the harvest, passed by with her maids. And it was she who Pluto saw as he was wounded by Cupid's arrow. Maddened with passion for Proserpine, Pluto grabbed her, and ignoring her desperate cries, sank with her into the fathomless abyss that was the Tartarus.

For several days, the goddess Ceres searched in vain for her beloved daughter. Finally, a water nymph told her what had happened. Overwhelmed with sorrow, Ceres cursed the earth for allowing Pluto to pass through it with Proserpine. Ceres' curse dried all the plants and the flowers and the earth was covered with ice.

Ceres then flew to Mount Olympus, the abode of the gods, and asked Jupiter to help her recover her daughter. Jupiter acceded, but told Ceres that he could only bring Proserpine back if she had not eaten anything during her stay in Tartarus. Unfortunately, Pluto, who was aware of Jupiter's agreement to help Ceres, offered a pomegranate to Proserpine and she ate it. The pomegranate was the fruit of the dead, and, by eating it, Proserpine was forever confined to remain in the Underworld. The most that Jupiter could do was convince Pluto to allow Proserpine to return to earth for half of the year. The other half she had to spend with Pluto.

As soon as Proserpine returned to earth, Ceres, filled with great joy, covered the planet with flowers. This marked the beginning of spring. During the half of the year that Proserpine stayed with her mother the earth was filled with warmth, flowers, and fruit. These were the spring and the summer seasons. But when Proserpine returned to Pluto, Ceres abandoned the earth. The leaves began to wither, the flowers were no longer abundant, and farmers began to gather their harvests. This was the autumn season, which was followed by winter, the most dreary of the periods on earth, when Ceres was most disconsolate for the absence of her daughter.

It is in the month of May, when flowers are most profuse and Mother's Day is celebrated, that Wicca observes Beltane, and the return of Proserpine to Ceres. Both Ceres and Proserpine are manifestations of the White Goddess among the Witches. Karnayna, her consort, represents Pluto.

In England, May 1 is celebrated by driving wooden poles adorned with colored ribbons into the ground. Young women take the ribbons and sing and dance around the May pole to symbolize the union of the male and the female principles.

The ceremony that is conducted during this festival is very simple. The High Priestess forms the Magic Circle and runs slowly around it, moving *deosil*, that is, clockwise. (The counterclockwise movement within the circle is known as *widdershins*.) The other Witches run after her as she sings the following:

> O, do not tell the priest about our art
> Because he would call it a sin,
> But we shall be in the woods all night
> A-conjuring summer in.
> And we shall bring glad tidings
> To woman, cattle, and corn
> For the Sun is coming up from the south
> With oak and ash and thorn.

In some covens, the High Priest recites the invocation known as Drawing Down the Moon, which we will discuss in chapter 4. During this invocation, the moon is called upon to descend upon the High Priestess. Afterwards, all the Witches eat of the fruit and cake offerings, drink sweet wine, and play their usual games.

June 21—Summer Solstice

This is one of the Witches' favorite festivals because the weather is warm and the rites may be held in the open if the participants wish. Many covens gather together to celebrate the ceremony.

The High Priestess casts the Circle. She stands in front of the cauldron, which has already been placed before the altar and filled with water. Many covens decorate the cauldron with flowers. The altar is set in the south.

The Witches surround the High Priestess, alternating men and women around the Circle. Behind the altar, on the north, stands the High Priest. Raising the magic wand, and still facing the altar and the High Priest, the High Priestess says:

Great Heavenly Being, power of the Sun
We invoke thee through the power of thine ancient names:
Michael, Balin, Arthur, Lugh, Herne.
Come again as of old to this thy land.
Lift up thy radiant spear and protect us.
Disperse the dark forces with thine overpowering light.
Grant us the gift of fragrant woods and green valleys,
Flowering orchards and tender corn.
Lead us to thy visionary mountain
And show us the lovely mansions of the gods.

The High Priestess raises her wand and traces a penta-gram in the air in front of the High Priest, who approaches the altar and picks up his wand, which rests upon it. He moves deosil around the altar and faces the cauldron, plung-ing the wand into the waters. He lifts up the cauldron and says:

> *The spear to the cauldron*
> *The lance to the Grail*
> *Spirit to flesh*
> *Man to woman*
> *Sun to Earth.*

The High Priest bows to the High Priestess and joins the rest of the coven. The High Priestess faces the coven and says:

> *Dance round the cauldron of Cerridwen, the goddess*
> *And be blessed by this consecrated water*
> *As the Sun, Lord of Life,*
> *Rises in all his might in the sign of the waters of life.*

She then proceeds to sprinkle some of the cauldron waters over the Witches. The coven dances around the altar led by the High Priest. Afterwards, they all sit down on the floor around the Circle and eat the offerings and drink the wine. As usual, games follow the eating and the drinking.

August 1—Lammas (Lugnasadah)

In ancient times, the Britons knew this day as the Feast of Bread. It was also known as the eve of Lady Day. It was a day where gratitude was expressed to the gods of nature for the grains of the harvests, specially the wheat from which bread is made. For that reason, it was a precursor of Thanksgiving, established by the pilgrims whose ancestry was mostly traced to England. The ancient Druids knew it as the fire festival of Lugnasadah, during which they lit bonfires in the fields to honor their gods.

Many covens celebrate Lammas with traditional dances around the Circle. The cauldron is filled with dry branches and magic herbs and placed in the south of the Circle, as the south represents the Fire element. As the cauldron is, lit the High Priest proceeds to Draw Down the Moon (see chapter 4). The High Priestess recites the Goddess' Charge, which we will discuss in chapter 5.

The male Witches kiss the High Priestess' feet and the female Witches bow to her. The High Priest gives white candles to all the members of the coven, who light them in the cauldron. They all walk slowly, deosil, around the Circle with their lit candles held high before them. The High Priest recites the following invocation:

> *Queen of the Moon.*
> *Queen of the Stars,*
> *Queen of the horns,*
> *Queen of Fire,*
>
> *Queen of Earth,*
> *Bring to us the child of promise*
> *For it is the Great Mother who gives birth to him.*
> *And it is the Lord of Life*
> *Who is born anew.*
> *Golden Sun of the mountains and the hills*

Illumine the world,
Illumine the seas,
Illumine the rivers,
Illumine all of us.
May sorrow perish and may joy be renewed!
Blessed be the Great Goddess
Without beginning and without end,
Everlasting to eternity!
Io Evo! He! Blessed Be!
Io Evo! He! Blessed Be!
Io Evo! He! Blessed Be!

The High Priest leads the coven in dances around the High Priestess, who represents the Great Goddess. Afterwards, they eat the fruits and the cakes and drink the wine, which are followed by more dances and games.

September 21—Autumn Equinox

At this time, when the earth begins to cover itself with a shroud of silence, farmers plant new seeds in their orchards and their fields. The planting of seeds is seen by the Witches as the beginning of the descent of Proserpine (the seed) towards the womb of the earth in her path to the Underworld. During the winter, the seeds lay dormant and in the spring they awaken into new life. The earth bursts asunder with green embryos, a symbol of renewed hope. For that reason, the Wiccan altars are adorned in this festival with pine cones, acorns, seeds, nuts, and fruits of the harvest, especially ear corns.

The High Priestess casts the Magic Circle and gives several lashes to the High Priest with her scourge to purify him. He purifies her in the same manner. The coven members purify each other, the male Witches using their scourges on the female Witches and vice versa. The High Priestess stands to the east of the Circle and the High Priest stands on the west, facing her. The High Priestess then says:

> Farewell, O Sun, ever-returning Light,
> The Hidden God, who nonetheless remains among us,
> Who now departs to the land of youth
> Through the gates of Death
> To dwell upon his throne, judge of gods and of humanity,
> The horned leader of the hosts of the air.
> And although he stands unseen in the midst of the Circle
> He carries within his being the secret seed,
> The seed of ripened grain, the seed of flesh;
> And although he is hidden in the bowels of the Earth,
> He also carries within him the wondrous seeds of the stars.
> Life is in him and life is the Light of humanity.
> He is that which was never born and never dies.
> Therefore, do not weep, Wicca, but rejoice.

It is clear in these words that Wicca, the Wise, are identified with Ceres, the Mother Earth, who awaits the return of the Sun in the springtime, and with the Sun, her beloved daughter, Proserpine. It is for this reason that Wicca is known as an earth religion, where earth and nature are worshipped in all their forms and all the yearly cycles. In this invocation, Pluto is identified with Proserpine because they represent the Male and the Female Principles from which everything proceeds. The Great Goddess, Aradia, and the Great God, Karnayna (they have other names), are the manifestation of these dual cosmic principles.

After the invocation, the coven salutes the Great God with dances around the Circle, which are repeated thrice. Cakes, fruits, wine and games follow.

October 31—All Hallow's Eve

This festival is better known in England and the United States as Halloween or Samhain. The Catholic Church observes November 1 as the Day of the Dead, and November 2 as All Saint's Day.

Halloween is another fire festival during which Witches invoke the spirits of the dead, who manifest their presences in the smoke of the cauldron.

This festival recognizes the formal end of summer when the power of dark forces is believed to increase. In ancient times, people used to secure their doors on this night and to place hollowed, lit pumpkins in their windows. The dual intention was to drive away evil spirits and to invite the souls of dead relatives to visit them. It was believed that on the stroke of midnight the souls of the dead were allowed to return to earth. Many Witches still observe these beliefs.

The custom of hollowing pumpkins and placing lit candles inside them is very common in the United States, where Halloween is extremely popular, albeit without its spiritual symbolism. Across the years, Halloween has become more like a costume party where children dress up as ghosts, ghouls, vampires, and other monsters of popular fiction. They go from house to house in their neighborhoods, carrying baskets and bags, demanding candies and toys, with the cry of "Trick or Treat." They are blissfully unaware that these same words were used in ancient times by other young people who also visited the houses of their neighbors looking for sweets. If they received a "treat" or sweets, they walked away satisfied. If they did not, they "tricked" the house owners with all sorts of nasty reprisals. They would stuff their chimneys, set loose their cattle, and squash the fruits of their orchards. In modern times, the "tricks" are not as costly but equally disagreeable, such as smashing eggs against windows and front doors.

To the Witches, Samhain (or Hallowmass as it is also known) is the most solemn and austere festival of the year.

In most covens, the ceremony begins with the purification of their members with the scourge. A red candle is lit in each of the four cardinal points of the room. The High Priestess places a wreath made of the flowers of the season upon the altar. She then casts the Circle and the coven members enter within. In the middle of the Circle, the cauldron is already flaming.

The High Priest says:

> *O gods, beloved by us,*
> *Bless our Great Sabbath*
> *So that we, thy humble servants,*
> *May celebrate this rite*
> *In love, joy and ecstasy.*
> *Bless our rite this night*
> *With the presence of our loved ones*
> *Who have already departed from the Earth.*

The Witches begin to walk slowly around the Circle, reciting the Runes, which we will discuss in a following chapter. The High Priest, on the west, and High Priestess, on the east, trace the pentagram in the air with their athames. Then the High Priestess calls the Great God to descend upon the High Priest with the following words:

Dread Lord of the Shadows,
God of Life, and the Giver of Life,
Open wide, I pray Thee, the Gates through which all must pass.
Let our dear ones who have gone before
Return this night to make merry with us.
And when our times comes, as it must,
O Thou, the Comforter, the Consoler,
the Giver of Peace and Rest,
We will enter thy realms gladly and unafraid;
For we know that when rested and refreshed
among our dear ones
We will be reborn again by thy grace,
and the grace of the Great Mother.
Let it be in the same place and the
same time as our beloved ones,
That we may meet, and know and remember,
And love them again.
Descend, we pray thee, on thy servant and priest.

All the female Witches give the Five-Fold Kiss to the High Priest, who is now the personification of the Great God. The High Priest kneels before the High Priestess, who places the flower wreath upon her head. Each member of the coven lights a red candle from those upon the altar and throws large quantities of incense upon the censer.

The High Priestess taps the ritual bell with her athame forty times and says:

> *Hearken to my words, O Witches.*
> *Be thou welcome to our Great Sabbath.*
> *Let us bid welcome together to the souls*
> *Of our departed ones.*

She again rings the bell with the athame forty times. The Witches begin to walk slowly, deosil, around the Circle. The High Priestess fills the ritual chalice with red wine and offers it to the High Priest. He sips the wine and says:

> *With all humility,*
> *And as the Great God commands,*
> *I ask my Witches to drink.*

He passes the chalice to one of the members of the coven with the right hand. With the left, he takes the coveners' red candle and plunges it into the wine. The Witch drinks some of the wine, which he then passes to the rest of the coven. When they have all drunk from the chalice, the High Priest says:

> *Harken, my Witches, to the words of the Great God:*
> *Drink, dance, and be merry*
> *In the presence of the ancient gods*
> *And the souls of our departed.*

The entire coven sits around the Circle and eat the offerings and drink more wine, inviting the souls of their dead ones to join in the food and drink. Then they concentrate on the flames on the cauldron, seeking within them the faces of their loved ones.

December 21—Winter Solstice (Yule)

To the Witches, the winter solstice is the true New Year. During this festival they celebrate the rebirth of the Sun God, who will die but will then be reborn.

The Romans celebrated the festival of the Saturnalia in honor of Saturn, who was the god of agriculture, on December 17. The festivities lasted until December 25, which included the winter solstice. At this time, they closed all their businesses, stopped all fighting and gave temporary freedom to their slaves. They spent all the days of the festival in a continuous celebration. Many Romans observed around the same time the festival of the god Mithra, worshipped in antiquity as the god of light. The Christian Churches, hoping to entice the pagans into their fold, chose December 25 as the Nativity or birth of Jesus. In this manner, many pagans identified Jesus with Mithra.

The ceremony of the winter solstice begins as always with the High Priestess casting the Magic Circle. She then invokes the presence of the Lords of the Watch Towers. The altar is adorned with mistletoe, pine branches, holly, and ivy.

All the lights are turned off and the room is lit by two candles on the altar. The cauldron is already ablaze in the south of the Circle. The cauldron's fire is fed by branches and dry leaves from nine different trees. Among them are cedar, elm, pine, juniper, elder, holly, and apple.

The High Priest Draws Down the Moon upon the High Priestess, who stands on the north, facing the cauldron. The Witches begin to walk, deosil, around the Circle, which is only lit by the cauldron's flames and the two candles. As the coven moves around the Circle, the High Priest lights candles in the cauldron and hands them to the Witches. When they all have lit candles in their hands, the High Priestess recites the same invocation used during the Lammas ritual. After the invocation, the Witches raise their candles and chant the following words over and over,

Io Evo! He! Io Evo! He!
Blessed Be! Blessed Be!

The High Priest then recites the Runes and takes the High Priestess by the hand. Together they jump over the cauldron's flames. The rest of the coven also jumps over the cauldron, in pairs. As they jump, they cry out,

Harrahya!

This word is also chanted at the end of the Runes, as we will see later.

The entire coven, led by the High Priest, passes in a long file in front of the High Priestess. The High Priest and all the male coveners kiss her on the right cheek. The women curtsy before her.

The High Priestess takes the chalice, which the High Priest fills with wine. She holds the chalice over the cauldron with both hands. The High Priest kneels down before her and plunges his athame into the wine. She drinks some of the wine and offers the chalice to the High Priest. He also drinks of the wine, and so do the other members of the coven. The last covener to drink from the chalice gives it to the High Priestess who drinks what is left of the wine.

The entire coven then lift their athames and point them to the four cardinal points, beginning on the north, which represents the Earth element.

The High Priest thanks the gods and the Lords of the Watch Towers for their presence during the ritual and dismisses them in the four quarters with the ritual words:

Hail and Farewell!

The ceremony ends, as usual, with fruits, cakes, wine, dances, and games.

3

THE IMPORTANCE OF THE MOON

Before we discuss the principal ceremony of Wicca it is necessary to delve into the relevance of the lunar phases in Witchcraft and in the practice of magic in general. As we all know, the moon has waxing and waning periods. The waxing moon begins with the new moon and culminates in the full moon. The waning phase begins with the full moon and ends with the new moon. The lunar cycle that starts and ends with the new moon lasts approximately twenty-eight days. Each of those twenty-eight days is known in Wicca and in Ceremonial Magic as a Lunar Mansion.

As it travels across the firmament in its orbit around the earth, the moon goes through each of the twelve zodiac signs, remaining around two days in each sign. The lunar influence on each sign has a profound effect on the earth and on human beings, and no one knows this better than Wicca. For this reason, Witches observe carefully these "lunar tides," which mark the signs that the moon is visiting day by day. The passage of the moon through the sign of Libra, for example, is used to cast love spells and conduct love rituals because Libra rules love and matrimony. If money is desired, the Witch waits until the moon is in the signs of Leo, Taurus, or Sagittarius. For business problems, the moon should be in Virgo or Capricorn. For health improvement, it should be in Leo. It is preferable that the moon be in a waxing phase as it passes through these signs because it has more light during that time. The waning moon is never used for any type of positive magic. It is used to dispel negative vibrations and to control enemies.

During its monthly cycle the moon goes through four different phases: first, second, third and fourth or last quarters.

First Quarter—This phase begins with the new moon, when the Sun and the moon are in conjunction, that is, they are in the same sign and in the same degree. The moon is not visible during the new moon because it rises at the same time as the Sun. The first quarter is used to start new projects and social activities, particularly those that favor the growth and expansion of ideas.

Second Quarter—This phase begins exactly in the middle between new moon and full moon, when the Sun and the moon are ninety degrees apart. This half moon rises around noon and sets around midnight. For this reason it may seen in the western sky during the early hours of the evening. The second quarter is also a period of growth and it is used to further things that have already started.

Third Quarter—This phase begins on full moon, when the Sun is directly opposite the moon and its rays illuminate the entire lunar orb. The full moon rises on the east as the Sun sets. After its Full phase, it rises progressively later each night. The effects of the full moon last twenty-four hours and it is a symbol of illumination, of the culmination of previous plans and what needs to be accomplished. It is the night preferred by Witches to conduct their rituals and cast spells because the abundance of lunar light makes any magic more powerful and effective. But the full moon is also a period when emotions are more difficult to control and there is a sense of unease; impulsive actions invariably lead to disaster at this time. Police precincts are usually on the alert during the full moon because many crimes and acts of violence are committed this night. That is why much wisdom must be used in every magic that is done on the full moon. The third quarter is therefore a period of maturity, fruition, and the most complete form of expression, both mental and spiritual. Many experienced Witches work very powerful magic during the third quarter.

Fourth (Last) Quarter—This phase begins halfway between full moon and new moon, when the Sun and the moon form a square aspect. For this reason, this period is not used for positive magic, such as spells for love or money. During this phase, the moon rises in the sky around midnight and may be seen on the eastern sky from that time onwards. It reaches the zenith or middle of the sky when the Sun rises. This is a period of disintegration, best used for reflection and reorganization. It is not a time for positive action on any level.

The night before the new moon, when it is totally devoid of light, is known among magical practitioners as the Dark moon. It is a tenebrous night when it is best to remain at home and avoid the streets, unless it is absolutely necessary. Witches believe that there are dark forces afoot on this night and their influence can be very destructive. It was precisely on the Dark Moon, twenty-four hours before the new moon, that Princess Diana was killed in an automobile accident. Diana was born under the sign of Cancer, ruled by the moon, and her name was that of the moon goddess among the Romans. For these reasons, Diana was more susceptible to the lunar tides than most people. The negative lunar influences of that night impacted strongly on her tragic death.

Following is a list of the moon as it passes through the twelve signs and what it influences in those days.

Moon in Aries—these are excellent days to start new things but they have little permanency due to Aries' volatile temperament. Things happen rapidly during this lunar aspect but also end with equal speed.

Moon in Taurus—everything that begins during this aspect is more stable and of greater duration. Businesses tend to do well when they are started with the Moon in Taurus. This aspect influences money and all financial matters strongly and its effect may be positive or negative, depending on whether the moon is waxing or waning.

Moon in Gemini—this lunar aspect affects all paperwork, contracts, studies and communications. Again, its influence may be positive or negative, depending on whether it is waning or waxing.

Moon in Cancer—this aspect affects the family, women, the mother, and trips, positively or negatively depending on its position. The moon in Cancer tends to stimulate communications and the feelings between people, making them stronger. It makes human issues more obvious and sensitive and nourishes emotional growth.

Moon in Leo—this aspect affects romance, children, entertainment, and money, positively or negatively. During this aspect people are more receptive to praise, and tend to become the center of attention and be rather melodramatic in their actions. There is an inclination towards recreational activities and to attend social functions.

Moon in Virgo—this aspect influences health, diets, and the organization of the home and business, positively or negatively. More attention is paid to details and there is an inclination towards perfectionism. People tend to be dictatorial during this period and a show of independence, either in word or action, is not well tolerated at home or at work.

Moon in Libra—love and marriage are deeply affected by this aspect, as well as associates, arts and pleasure, either on a positive or a negative manner. People are more self conscious and aware of their actions. This aspect favors automatic discrimination and interaction with other people, but it is not favorable to spontaneous initiative.

Moon in Scorpio—this aspect affects human sexuality and exacerbates jealous tendencies and distrust. These influences are less impacting if the moon is waxing but worsen if it is waning. The waxing Moon in Scorpio is excellent to pursue the development of psychic abilities. One of its most dramatic influences is the tendency to sever personal relationships. All relationships that terminate when the moon is in Scorpio are permanent. That is why it is advised to avoid arguments or personal confrontations during this lunar aspect.

Moon in Sagittarius—if the moon is waxing, this aspect brings abundance, prosperity, money, and expansion; if it is waning, it brings financial restrictions. The Moon in Sagittarius affects superiors at the job place, judges, bank officials, and persons in authority or positions of power, who will be magnanimous if the moon is waxing and less than helpful if it is waning. This aspect lends itself to expansionism, flights of fancy, and self-assurance.

Moon in Capricorn—if the moon is waxing, it will affect in a positive manner all matters concerning agriculture, inheritances, real state, and old people. If it is waning it will incline towards pessimism, caution and the desire to plan each action meticulously. People tend to be more disciplined and better organized when the moon is in Capricorn. They do not take unnecessary chances and every important decision is carefully calculated.

Moon in Aquarius—this lunar aspect is diametrically opposed as the Moon in Capricorn. The tendencies are towards eccentricity and everything that is daring and innovative. It is a period during which impulsive actions are carried out, without considering their possible outcomes. Aquarius is an explosive and volatile sign which rules technology and the atom bomb. The moon, which is voluble and changeable, multiplies these characteristics making this aspect a dangerous period if control is not exercised every step of the way. The position of the moon affects these tendencies powerfully, making them more explosive if it is waning.

Moon in Pisces—this aspect inclines towards mysticism, meditation, and auto-introspection. But it also inclines towards excesses in the use of alcohol and drugs. For this reason it is extremely important to curtail the use of alcoholic beverages and drugs during this period. People tend to be more sensitive and more inclined towards idealism and spirituality. Dreams are often prophetic during this aspect. Pisces is very susceptible to outside influences and it is often exploited by others. When the moon is in Pisces, it is important to avoid forceful persons and postpone the lending of money, until the moon leaves the sign and the mind is clear and more focused on material things. The waning moon increases the negative influences of this aspect.

The easiest way to learn the monthly lunar aspects, and to know when it is waning or waxing, is to have at hand an astrological calendar that provides this information.

As we already saw, the moon remains two days in each sign, which makes it possible to delay important decisions affecting specific circumstances until the moon is waxing in the appropriate sign. Witches only do their magic when the moon is in the sign that rules the subject they wish to influence.

Another lunar aspect of great importance in the practice of magic is the period when the moon is "void-of-course." This information can also be found in an astrological calendar.

When the moon is void-of-course it is very unstable and nothing new should be started as it will fail to be fully realized. The moon is void-of-course when it forms the last aspect with one of the planets that is in the sign visited by the moon. From that moment until the moon leaves the sign and enters the next, it is said to be out of course, that is, it has no trajectory. For example, if the moon forms a trine or a square with Mercury in the sign of Cancer, and that is its last aspect while it remains in Cancer, it goes out of course at that moment. It will be out of course until it leaves Cancer to enter the next sign, which is Leo. This period lasts only a few hours but those hours are of primordial importance in every human action, especially in the practice of magic because during that time the moon has no direction and everything that is done then will be void and null. That is the reason why many magic are not successful. If the person who does the magic does not have sufficient knowledge of the lunar tides, including the moon void-of-course, he or she will be disappointed when the magic fails. In rituals of invocation or Evocation, when a spirit is called to manifest physically in front of the Magician, it is also important to observe the Sun sign and the aspects between planets so that the ceremony will be effective.

The position of the moon and its aspects are of tremendous importance in Wicca. No spell or ceremony will be conducted before ascertaining the lunar and planetary influences.

4

THE MAJOR CEREMONY OF WICCA AND THE GREAT RITE

The first thing that a Witch learns is how to cast and consecrate the Magic Circle which not only serves as a protection against negative forces but also helps concentrate energies during the rituals. To cast and consecrate the Circle, the Witch needs several implements: the ceremonial black-handled knife known as the athame; the pentacle, which is a disk of copper, silver, or wood, about six inches in diameter and engraved with the Wiccan symbols; uniodized salt; a small receptacle of water and a sprinkler; a censer with burning charcoals and incense; and four candleholders with four white candles.

The ideal dimensions of the Circle are nine feet in diameter, but this can be altered if the coven is very large or if the ceremony is conducted in the open. Any of the members of the coven may trace the Circle, but usually it is the High Priestess who carries out this task.

The four candles are placed in the four cardinal points. If the ceremony is conducted indoors, all the lights are usually turned off so that the room is illuminated only by the candles. The altar, a table with two white candles, is positioned in the north of the room because Witches work their magic from that cardinal point, which represents the Earth element. That is one of the reasons why Wicca is known as an earth religion.

The incense is lit and placed upon the altar. At this moment, the High Priestess consecrates the water. She places the water receptacle over the Pentacle, dips the tip of the athame in the liquid, and says:

I exorcise thee, O creature of water, that thou cast out from thee all impurities and uncleanliness of the spirits of the world of phantasm. In the names of Aradia and Karnayna.

She sets the water aside and pours some salt over the Pentacle. She places the point of the athame over the salt and says:

Blessings be upon this creature of salt. Let all malignity and hindrance be cast henceforth, and let all good enter herein. But ever mind, water purifies the body, but the scourge purifies the soul. Wherefore I bless thee, that thou may aid me, in the names of Aradia and Karnayna.

After she has exorcised the salt, she pours it into the water, which is now deemed blessed water. She then points the athame towards the north point and begins to move deosil, tracing an invisible circle in the air, from north to east, from east to south, from south to west, and from west to north. The deosil movement, always to the right, imitates the motion of the Sun and the hands of the clock. It is always used in rituals of White Magic. Widdershins, the movement to the left, is often used in Black Magic, although some times it is used in White Magic for specific purposes.

Once the Circle has been cast, no one may move Widder-shins within it.

As the High Priestess casts the Circle, she says:

I conjure thee, O circle of power, that thou be a boundary between the material world and the world of the Mighty Ones, a guardian and protector that shall preserve and contain the power that we shall raise within it. Wherefore do I bless and consecrate thee.

When the High Priestess begins to cast the Circle with the athame, she traces an invisible portal with it in the Northeast, so that the other members of the coven may enter the Circle after it has been consecrated. After they have all entered, she seals that astral doorway and the Circle is closed.

As soon as the Circle is cast, the High Priestess sprinkles it with the blessed water from north to north. She then passes the incense, followed by a lit candle, also from north to north. This purifies the Circle with the four elements: Water, Earth (salt), Air (incense), and Fire (the candle).

After the Circle has been purified, the High Priestess stands in the east and traces a pentagram in the air with the point of the athame. As you can see in the accompanying diagram, the pentagram may be traced from the bottom to the top, from the top to the bottom, left to right or right to left. Each pentagram form is associated with one of the four elements plus a fifth element, known as Ether or Spirit. This fifth element is also known in Ceremonial Magic as Akasha.

There are two types of pentagram, invocation, and vanishing. The Earth Invoking Pentagram is used at the beginning of every magical ceremony and is the one used by the High Priestess when she casts the Circle. The Earth Vanishing Pentagram is used to vanish the Circle after the ceremony has concluded. As I mentioned earlier, the pentagram is a new addition to Wicca and originates in Kabbalistic teachings associated with Ceremonial Magic (see figures on page 58).

As she traces the Invoking Pentagram of the Earth element in the air, the High Priestess says:

O Lords of the Watch Towers of the east, I call and conjure thee so that thou may be witnesses of my ritual and guard the Circle.

She points to the center of the invisible pentagram with the athame, kisses the blade, and places it over her heart. She repeats the same invocation on the south, west, and north, calling upon the Lords of the Watch Towers of those cardinal points, pointing the athame, kissing the blade, and placing it over her heart each time.

The Lords of the Watch Towers are spirits of immense power, associated with the angels. The pentagrams and the Invocations commence in the east because all the spirits of light are invoked starting at that point. When the invocation starts in the west, the spirits invoked are invariably forces of darkness. The circle is cast from north to north because the Wiccan ceremony is conducted on the material world, represented by the Earth element, but the spirits are always invoked from east to east.

Before the High Priestess invokes the Lords of the Watch Towers the entire coven has already been admitted into the Circle. The first who enters is the High Priest, who is greeted by the High Priestess with a kiss on the left cheek. She turns him around once and places him behind her. When the rest of the coven enters the Circle, the High Priest kisses the women on the left cheek and the High Priestess does the same with the men.

Each time the High Priestess invokes the Lords of the Watch Towers all the coveners raise their athames and point them towards the various cardinal points, following the High Priestess' lead.

After the Lords of the Watch Towers have been invoked, the High Priest Draws Down the Moon on the High Priestess. The moon, in this case, represents the Great Goddess or Cosmic Mother.

The High Priestess stands in the north, in the "god position." In this position, her feet are placed side by side and her arms are crossed over her breast. In one hand she holds the athame and in the other, the ritual scourge.

The High Priest gives her the Five-Fold Kiss, kneels before her, and proceeds to recite the invocation known as Drawing Down the Moon:

> *I invoke thee and call upon thee, O Mighty Mother of us all,*
> *Bringer of all fruitfulness;*
> *By seed and root, by bud and stem,*
> *By leaf and flower and fruit,*
> *By life and love do we invoke thee*
> *To descend upon the body of thy servant and Priestess.*

The High Priest and all the men present kiss the High Priestess on the right cheek. The women curtsy to her, passing in front of her, one by one. The High Priestess traces the Invoking Pentagram of Earth in front of her and says:

> *Of the Mother darksome and divine*
> *Mine the scourge and mine the kiss,*
> *The five-point star of love and bliss.*
> *Here I charge you with this sign.*

She then assumes the "goddess position," opening her arms on each side and spreading her feet. In this stance she forms a pentagram with her body.

The High Priest says:

> *Hearken to the words of the Great Mother, who in ancient times was known by many names: Artemis, Astarte, Dione, Melusine, Aphrodite, Diana, Cerridwen, Dana, Arianrhod, Isis and many others. Upon her altars, the youth of Lacedaemon in Sparta offered her due sacrifice.*

At this moment the High Priestess recites the Charge of the Goddess, which we will discuss with the Runes in the next chapter.

After the High Priestess recites the Charge, the coven proceeds to raise the Cone of Power. To do this they form a circle, alternating men and women, holding hands. The High Priestess and High Priest are also part of the Circle. The begin to walk deosil, slowly at first and then with increasing speed as they recite the Runes. This raises huge quantities of energy. The coven continues to move rapidly around the Circle until they are finally running. As they run, they chant the last part of the Runes:

Eko, Eko Azarak
Eko, Eko, Samilak
Eko, Eko Karnayna
Eko, Eko, Aradia
Bezabi, Lacha, Bachababa
Lamach, Caji, Achababa
Karrelos, Caji, Achababa
Lamach, Lamach, Bachabarous
Carbaji, Sabalios, Barilos
Lazoz, Athame, Caliolas
Samajac et Famiolas
Harrahyah

When the High Priestess senses that enough energy has been raised and that the Cone of Power has been erected in the middle of the Circle, she stops the coven with a last cry of "Harrahyah!" At this moment the Witches use the energies within the Cone to carry out the magical work of the evening. This may consist of spell casting, visualizations, healings, or the favorite magic of most Witches, the magic cord, which we will discuss in another chapter.

If a Sabbath or major holiday is celebrated that night, that ritual is added to the ceremony after the Charge. Only then is the Cone of Power raised by the coven.

After the magical work is finished, they all sit around the Circle, eat the fruits and cake and drink the wine as usual. All the offerings are consecrated and purified by the High Priestess before their consumption. To do this, she stands again in the position of the god, feet together, arms crossed over her breast, the athame in her right hand and the scourge on her left. The High Priest kisses her feet and her knees and kneels before her, head bowed. He then fills the chalice with red wine and raises it before the High Priestess, always with bowed head. She places the tip of the athame inside the chalice and says:

As the athame represents the man, so does the chalice represent the woman, and together they bring joy.

She drinks some of the wine and gives the chalice to the High Priest who passes it on to the rest of the coven. All the Witches drink of the wine and return the chalice to the High Priestess who drinks what is left.

The High Priest presents the pentacle, where the cakes have been placed, to the High Priestess. When he presents the pentacle he says:

O Goddess, the most secret, bless Thou these offerings in our bodies, granting us energy, strength and power, peace and joy and that love which is the eternal joy of human beings.

The High Priestess touches the offerings with the tip of the athame and blesses them. She then eats one of the cakes. The High Priest also eats a cake and passes the rest to the coven. If there are more offerings, they are all blessed in the same manner, which they eat while sitting around the Circle. The various games are then played. When they are ended, the High Priestess returns to the Circle and proceeds to discharge the Lords of the Watch Towers using the Vanishing Pentagram of the Earth element, tracing it this time from top to bottom. She starts at the east, and, after tracing the Vanishing Pentagram, says:

O Lords of the Watch Towers of the east, I thank Thee for Thy presence during this ceremony and ere Thou depart to Thy lovely realms I say, Hail and Farewell.

She points to the center to the pentagram, kisses the athame's blade and places it over her breast. She repeats the same actions in the other three cardinal points, but addressing the Lords of the Watch Towers according to the quarter to which they belong. She then points the tip of the athame towards the north and walks deosil around the Circle, returning to the north once more. She says:

The circle is now vanished and the ritual has ended.

The candles are put out, without blowing on them, in the same order in which they were lit. The lights are turned on again and the High Priestess proceeds to ring the bell ten times and the entire coven stamp their feet on the floor ten times also, to signify their return to the material world. The water that is left, and the ashes in the censer, are disposed of. The candles are put away to be used in the next ceremony. All the Witches pick up their ritual implements and kiss each other on the right cheek saying:

Merry meet and merry part. Blessed be.

This is the end of the main ceremony of Wicca which is celebrated during every Esbat or Sabbath.

The Great Rite

This ceremony is secret and very ancient and it is rarely used by modern covens. It consists of the sexual act between the High Priest and High Priestess, who are often married. The Great Rite is never celebrated in public, but in private, after the ceremony has ended. It was used in ancient times to ratify a magical act of great importance, uniting in this manner the male and female principles represented by Aradia and Karnayna. It is similar to the rite of Tantric Yoga and it is considered an act of universal love between two highly spiritual human beings who love each other deeply. In most modern covens, where the High Priest and High Priestess are not married, the Great Rite is not carried out. Many modern Witches consider it unnecessary because the joined work of the coven is sufficiently powerful and dynamic, and does not need the sexual energies of any of its members. The rite is mentioned here because in ancient times it was an intrinsic part of Wicca and it is therefore a part of its history and tradition.

5

THE RUNES AND THE CHARGE

As we saw in the preceding chapter, the Runes are undoubt edly one of the most important parts of the Wiccan ceremony, during which the Witches raise the Cone of Power. These are the Runes:

> *Darksome night and shining moon,*
> *east, then south, then west, then north,*
> *Hearken to the Witches' Runes.*
> *Here I come to call thee forth,*
> *Earth and Water, Air and Fire,*
> *Wand and pentacle and sword,*
> *Work ye unto my desire.*
> *Hearken ye unto my word.*
> *Cords and censer, scourge and knife,*
> *Powers of the Witch's blade,*
> *Waken all ye unto life,*
> *Come ye as the charm is made.*
> *Queen of heaven, Queen of hell,*
> *horned hunter of the night,*

lend your power unto my spell
and work my will by magic rite.
By all the power of land and sea,
By all the might of moon and sun,
As I do will, so mote it be.
Chant the spell, and be it done.
Eko, eko azarak
Eko, eko zamilak
Eko, Eko Karnayna
Eko, eko Aradia.
Bezabi, lacha bachababa
Lamach, caji, achababa
Karrelos, caji, achababa
Lamach, lamach bacharous
Carbajayi, sabalios, barilos
Lazo, athame, caliolas
Samajac et famiolas.
Harrahyah!

The verses that begin with Eko, Eko Azarak and end in Harrahyah are repeated as the Witches run around the Circle to raise the Cone of Power. The High Priestess decides when the Runes are to be ended, reciting the last "Harrahyah." The Runes are chanted, alternating in a low and a loud voice. It is the most impressive of the Wiccan ceremonies, and many people claim to have actually seen the Cone of Power rising like a pyramid in the center of the Circle as the Runes are chanted.

The Charge

The Charge is a call to the Great Goddess, also known as the White Goddess, who is identified with the moon, the forces of nature and with the Cosmic Mother. Through the Charge, the Great Goddess instructs the Witches, her children, in the perfect manner in which to adore her and do homage unto her. The Charge is always a part of the Wiccan traditional ceremony and is recited by the High Priestess, who represents the Great Goddess. The High Priest assists the High Priestess during this impressive ritual. This is the Goddess' Charge:

High Priest: Hearken now to the words of the Great Goddess, who was known in ancient times as Artemis, Astarte, Athena, Dione, Melusine, Aphrodite, Cerridwen, Diana, Arianrhod, Isis and many other names. Upon her altars, the youth of Lacedaemon in Sparta, made duly sacrifices in her honor.

High Priestess: Whenever ye have need of anything, once a month and better it be when the moon is full, then shall ye assemble in some secret place, and adore the spirit of me, who am Queen of all Witches.

There shall ye assemble, ye who are fain to learn all sorcery, yet have not won its deepest secrets, to these will I teach things that are as yet unknown.

And ye shall be free from slavery; and as a sign that ye be really free, ye shall be naked in your rites; and ye shall dance, sing, feast, make music and love, all in my praise. For mine is the ecstasy of the spirit, and mine is also joy on Earth; for my law is love unto all beings.

Keep pure your highest ideal; strive ever towards it; let naught stop you or turn you aside; for mine is the secret door which opens upon the door of youth, and mine is the cup of the wine of life, and the cauldron of Cerridwen, which is the Holy Grail of immortality.

I am the gracious Goddess, who gives the gift of joy unto the heart of man. Upon Earth, I give the knowledge of the spirit eternal; and beyond death, I give peace and freedom, and reunion with those who have gone before.

Nor do I demand sacrifice, for behold I am the Mother of all living, and my love is poured upon the Earth.

High Priest: Hearken to the words of the Star Goddess; the heavenly host dwell at her feet and her body surrounds the entire universe.

High Priestess: I am the beauty of the green Earth; the white moon among the stars; and the desire in every human heart. Call upon mine soul; rise and come unto me, for I am the soul of nature and I give life to the universe. All things proceed from me and to me they shall all return. Before mine face, beloved of gods and men, let the divinity of thy beings be embraced in the ecstasy of the Infinite. Let the adoration of mine spirit vibrate in thine hearts because all acts of love and pleasure are my rituals. Therefore let there be beauty, strength, power, compassion, honor, humility, joy, and reverence in thy beings.

And thou, who thinkest to seek for me, know thy seeking
and yearning will avail thee not unless thou know the mystery:
that if that which thou seekest findest not within thee,
thou will never find it without thee. For behold,
I have been with thee from the beginning,
and I am that which is attained at the end of desire.

Wicca's Symbol

Invocation   Banishing   Invocation   Banishing

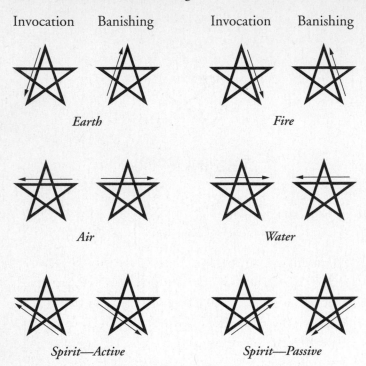

Earth   *Fire*

Air   *Water*

Spirit—Active   *Spirit—Passive*

* Pentagrams of the four elements: Earth, Fire, Air, and Water, and of the fifth element of Spirit, Ether (Akasha).

6

THE INITIATIONS

All aspirant Witches must be initiated into the mysteries of the religion. Wicca has three traditional initiations: First, Second, and Third Degree, which is the highest. When Witches achieve the Third Degree, they can leave the coven and start their own group, if they so desire. Only Third Degree Initiates can aspire to the title of High Priest or High Priestess.

First Degree Initiation

This is the first initiation received by the aspirant Witch. After the initiation, he or she is accepted as a member of the coven and must always render homage to the High Priest and High Priestess who lead it.

During the First Degree Initiation, only the High Priest and Priestess are present in the room where the ritual takes place. Sometimes the Maiden, who is the High Priestess' assistant, is also present. The rest of the coven awaits the conclusion of the initiation in another room.

The initiation begins with the main ceremony of Wicca, which we discussed in chapter 4. The aspirant Witch, who has undergone a ritual bath, enters the Circle through the astral door traced by the High Priestess in the northeast. In most covens, the aspirant Witch is naked during the ritual, although some covens allow the person to wear clothes, usually a black tunic. The person is blindfolded.

The High Priestess places the point of the athame on the chest of the person and says:

O thou who standest on the threshold between the material world and the realms of the dread Lords of the outer spaces, hast thou the courage to make the assay?

The initiate says:

I have.

The High Priestess continues:

For verily I say unto thee that it were better to rush on my blade and perish, than to make the attempt with fear in thine heart.

The initiate answers:

I have two words.

High Priestess:

Which are those words?

Initiate:

Perfect love and perfect trust.

High Priestess:

All who have those words are doubly welcome. And I give thee a
third, to bring thee luck inside the Circle.

As she says these words, she kisses him lightly upon the
lips and guides him to the south of the Circle, where she ties
a cord to his right ankle, saying:

The feet are neither free nor bound.

She then uses another, much longer cord, to tie the initiate's hands behind his back. She takes a length of the cord,
ties it loosely around his hands, and lets what is left dangle
over his chest.

This is the part of the ceremony that demands the initiate's maximum confidence in the High Priest and High
Priestess, as he is blindfolded, hands tied behind his back,
and a cord around his neck. He is literally incapacitated to
defend himself if the two persons upon whom he has
entrusted his life decide to do him any physical harm. That is
why the two words are "perfect love and perfect trust." The
initiate has perfect trust that the ceremony in which he is par-
ticipating is a test of love and not of torture.

The High Priestess holds her athame with her right hand
and with her left she takes the cord that hangs over the initiate's breast and pulls him towards the east of the Circle. She
points the athame upwards and says:

Take heed, ye Lords of the Watch Towers of the east, that (here
she says the name of the initiate) is properly prepared to be
made a priest and a Witch of the Goddess.

She repeats the same call in the south, west and north,
but invoking the lords of those quarters. She pulls the initiate
by the cord to bring him to each cardinal point. She then

places her left arm around his waist and runs deosil with him three times around the Circle. When they are back in the east she rings the bell eleven times and says:

In other religions the postulant kneels, while the priest towers above him; but in the art magical we are taught to be humble, so we kneel to welcome them and we say,
Blessed be thy feet that have brought thee in these ways.

(She kneels and kisses first his right foot, then his left.)

Blessed be thy knees that shall kneel at the sacred altar.

(She kisses both knees.)

Blessed be thy belly that holds the seed of life.

(She kisses his belly.)

Blessed be thy breast, formed in strength and beauty.

(She kisses both breasts.)

Blessed be thy lips that shall utter the sacred names.

(She kisses his lips.)

This is the Five-Fold Kiss which we have already discussed. She then says:

Before thou art sworn, art thou willing
to pass the test and be purified?

The initiate answers "yes," and she proceeds to take his magical measurements with a red cord. First she measures his head with the end of the cord and marks it with a knot; from this knot she measures his chest and makes another knot; then she measures his hips, tying the third knot; and finally she measures his height, making the last knot. She then says:

In the old days, at the same time the measure was taken, hair and nail clippings would have been taken from you too, and put with your measure in a secret place. Then if you tried to leave the coven, the coven would use them to bring you back, and you would never break away. But because you came into our circle with two perfect words, perfect love and perfect trust, we give you your measure back.

She secures the cord around the initiate's left arm. She then ties the cord around his right ankle to the left ankle and helps him to kneel, with his head bowed near his knees. She rings the bell three times, tapping it with the athame, and proceeds to lash the initiate's back forty times with the scourge. The lashes are divided in four groups: first three lashes, then seven, then nine, and finally twenty-one lashes. Wicca's scourge is symbolic and the strips that form it are usually made of silk and do not harm the initiate.

After the ritual scourging, the High Priestess says:

Thou hast bravely passed the test. Art thou ready to swear that thou wilt always be true to the Art, and ever ready to protect, help, and defend thy brothers and sisters of the Wicca, even though it should cost thee thy life?

The initiate answers "yes," and the High Priestess continues:

Then repeat after me Wicca's oath: "I (name), in the presence of the Mighty Ones, do of my own free will and accord most solemnly swear that I will ever keep secret, and never reveal, the secrets of the Art, except it be to a proper person, properly prepared within a circle such as I am now in. All this I swear by my hopes of a future life, mindful that my measure has been taken; and may my weapons turn against me if I break this my sacred oath."

The initiate repeats these words after the High Priestess, who then helps him rise, unties the cords that bind him, and removes the blindfold.

The initiate blinks in the dim light of the candles and sees the High Priestess smiling gently at him. She opens a small bottle filled with consecrated oil and forms an inverted triangle on the body of the new Witch with a finger dipped in the oil. To form the triangle, she touches her finger to his right breast, then to his left breast, and finally to his abdomen. As she forms the triangle, she says:

I consecrate thee with oil.

She forms a second triangle in the same manner, but this time with red wine from the chalice, saying:

I consecrate thee with wine.

She then kisses the three points of the triangle, saying:

I consecrate thee with my lips, priest and Witch.

The new Witch is then presented with the magical weapons or implements of the Art by the High Priestess, who says:

I now present thee with the working tools of a Witch. First, the magic sword. With this, as with the athame, thou canst trace the Magic Circle, subdue and punish rebellious spirits. With it in your hand, thou art the master of the Magic Circle. Next I present thee with the athame, or black-handled knife. This is the true Witch's weapon and has the same powers as the magic sword. Next I present thee with the bolline or white-handled knife. Its use is to form and inscribe all instruments used in the Art. It can only be used inside the Magic Circle. Next I present thee with the magic wand. Its purpose is to call forth certain genii and spirits to whom it would not be meet to use the sword

*or athame. Next I present thee with the pentacle which has
many uses, including the invocation of certain spirits. And here
is the censer, which is used to attract good spirits and banish
evil ones. And here is the scourge, a symbol of power and domi-
nation, of suffering and purification, for it is written, to learn
thou must learn to suffer and be purified. Art thou willing to
suffer to learn?*

The new Witch says "yes," and the High Priestess continues:

*Lastly, I present thee with the cords which are used to bind the
sigils or seals of the Art and in every oath.*

(There are three cords: blue, red, and white; of these, blue
is the one most commonly used.)

*And now I salute thee in the name of Aradia and Karnayna,
new priest and Witch.*

Each time that the High Priestess hands one of the magic
weapons to the initiate she kisses him on the right cheek. He
passes the weapons to the Maiden who places them on the
altar.

The High Priestess then leads the initiate to the east,
points upwards with the athame and says:

*Hearken to my words, O powerful beings, this initiate (name)
has been consecrated in the Art and as brother of Wicca.*

She repeats the same words in the other three cardinal
points. At this moment, the rest of the coven enters the Circle
through the astral portal traced by the High Priestess on the
northeast. They all drink wine from the chalice and celebrate
the initiation with fruits, cakes, and games as usual.

It is important to know that the initiations in Wicca are given man to woman and woman to man. If the initiate is a man, the High Priestess performs the ceremony. If it is a woman, then it is the High Priest who conducts the initiation. In certain cases, a mother may initiate her daughter and the father his son, but these ceremonies are only conducted in very special circumstances.

Before he undergoes the initiation, the aspirant Witch chooses a magical name which is always used among the coven. The Second Degree Initiation also requires another name, but this is only used in major rituals. In the Third Degree Initiation, the female Witches receive one of the secret names of the Great Goddess and the males one of the secret names of the Great God.

Second Degree Initiation

The High Priest, High Priestess, and the Witches who have received this initiation are all present during the ceremony. The High Priestess traces the Magic Circle. Let us imagine that it is a female Witch who will receive the initiation. The High Priest performs the ritual. The initiate enters the Circle, already washed and purified, with her hands tied behind her back, but not blindfolded. Beginning at the east, the High Priest proclaims on the four quarters:

Hearken unto my words, O Mighty Ones, behold (name), a Priestess and Witch already consecrated, who has been prepared for the elevation to the Second Degree.

Placing his arm around the initiate's waist, the High Priest runs with her three times around the Circle. The initiate then kneels before the altar and her ankles are bound. The High Priest, who is facing her, says:

> *To receive this Degree thou must be purified.*
> *Art thou willing to suffer to learn?*

The Witch says "yes," and the High Priest continues:

> *I purify thee so that thou wilt make the oath correctly.*

He rings the bell three times and lashes the Witch forty times with the scourge in the four groups of lashings already mentioned: three, seven, nine, and thirty-one. He then says:

> *Repeat after me: "I (magical name of the Witch), swear on my*
> *mother's womb and my honor among men and my Brothers*
> *and Sisters in the Art, that I shall never reveal the secrets of the*
> *Art, except to proper persons prepared in a Magic Circle as I am*
> *now in. This I swear on my past lives and my hopes for future*
> *lives and I devote myself and my measure to utter destruction if*
> *I break this my solemn oath."*

The High Priest kneels beside the initiate, places his left hand behind her knees and his right hand over her head. He says:

> *I will all my power unto thee.*

He helps her stand up and unties the cords that bind her. With the tip of his finger, dipped in consecrated oil, he forms a pentagram on her body. He begins by touching his finger to her abdomen, then to her right foot, her left knee, her right knee, her left foot, and once again the abdomen. When he finishes tracing the pentagram, he says:

> *I consecrate thee with oil.*

He then repeats the pentagram and the words of consecration with wine, water, fire (a lit candle), and a kiss on each point of the pentagram. He gives the Witch her weapons, already used, and invites her to use them in the Circle. The Witch traces the Circle with her magic sword and then with the athame. She uses the white-handled knife to inscribe a pentagram in one of the candles that lay on the altar and which she will use at the proper time in her own coven. She points the magic wand in the direction of the four quarters, presents the pentacle in the four directions and passes the censer around the Circle. As she reuses her weapons she passes them to the High Priest who kisses them and places them on the altar. Finally, the High Priest gives her the magic cords and orders her to tie him with them. The Witch obeys and the High Priest kisses her on the right cheek, saying:

Thou must learn that in Wicca thou must ever give as thou receive, but ever triple. I gave thee three, return nine; I gave thee seven, return twenty-one; I gave thee nine, return twenty-seven; I gave thee twenty-one, return sixty-three. These make 120 lashings. Here is the scourge.

The Witch obeys and strikes the High Priest 120 times with the scourge. He then unties the cords that bind her, kisses her on the right cheek and says:

Thou hast obeyed the Law. When thou receive good, thou must return the good three times.

This oath, based on the Law of Three, forces every Second Degree Witch to return evil for evil and good for good thrice to the person from whom he receives it. This makes the Witch a powerful enemy because he or she is obligated by the laws of Wicca to seek revenge. He or she is also the best friend one may have because of the Law of Three.

After the scourging, the Witch is presented to the four cardinal points by the High Priest, who says:

Hail, O Mighty Ones, this initiate (name) has been properly elevated to the Second Degree.

From this moment onwards the Witch is considered a High Priestess, but she cannot start her own coven. She must wait until she receives the Third Degree Initiation before she is allowed to leave the mother coven.

After the initiation has ended, the coven eats the fruits and the cakes and carry on their games as usual.

The Third Degree Initiation

Only the High Priest, the High Priestess, and the Witches who have received this initiation may be present at the ceremony. This means that the group of Witches will be smaller because not every member has gone beyond the Second Degree.

This is one of the most beautiful and complex of the Wiccan ceremonies because during the ritual the abduction of Proserpine (the Great Goddess) by Pluto (the Great God) is related and dramatized. The High Priestess acts the part of the Great Goddess and the High Priest that of the Great God. Also present within the Circle is the narrator of this odyssey, who is also a Third Degree initiate. All the participants are doubly purified before the ritual.

The circle is cast in the usual manner and the main ceremony is carried out, including the Drawing Down the Moon upon the High Priestess. After the main ceremony, the High Priestess divests herself of her ritualistic necklace, which is made of alternating amber and jet beads, and lays it upon the altar. She then places a long, transparent veil over her head which covers her entire body. She wears several ritualistic jewels on her hands and arms. Her ritual crown remains upon her head.

The High Priest places his horned crown on his head and places the magic sword on a belt around his waist. Thus attired, he stands before the altar in the position of the Great God, feet together and hands crossed over his chest. As he does this, he pulls the sword from his belt and holds it in his right hand. The scourge is in his left hand. The High Priestess leaves the Circle through the astral portal in the northeast and stands outside the Circle. Another Witch, also a Third Degree initiate, stands by the astral doorway. He represents the guardian of Pluto's realm.

The narrator of the gods' odyssey says:

In ancient times, our Lord, he of the great horned head, was as he still is, Counselor and Benefactor; but men only knew him as the dread Lord of Darkness, solitary, severe but just. Our Lady, the Great Goddess, wished to solve all mysteries, even the mystery of Death. For this reason, she descended to the kingdom in the depths of the Earth, but the guardian of the doorway barred her path.

At this point, the High Priestess, who acts as the Great Goddess, approaches the Witch who guards the astral portal. But he, who represents the guardian of the Great God's realm, stops her, and points his sword at her breast, saying:

Divest thyself of thy raiment, set aside thy jewels, for thou mayest not bring aught with thee into our kingdom.

Narrator:

> *And she set aside her raiment and her jewels*
> *and was bound, as all must be bound*
> *who attempt to enter the Kingdom of Death,*
> *the realm of the Mighty Ones.*

The High Priestess removes her veil and her jewels and places them on the floor, outside the Circle. The guardian of the portal ties her with cords and brings her into the Circle.

Narrator:

> *And her beauty was so great that Death himself*
> *knelt down and placed his sword*
> *and his crown on the dust, and kissed her feet.*

The High Priest approaches the High Priestess, looks at her as if transfixed, and kneels before her. He places his sword and his crown on the floor, kisses her feet, and says:

> *Blessed by thy feet*
> *which have brought thee here.*
> *Remain by my side and let me*
> *place my icy hand over thy breast.*

High Priestess:

> *I do not love thee.*

High Priest:

> *Then, if thou wilt not receive*
> *My hand upon thy heart,*
> *Thou must kneel*
> *To receive Death's punishment.*

High Priestess:

> *It is fate, better be so.*

She kneels before the High Priest and he strikes her forty times with the scourge.

Narrator:

> *And Death stroke her tenderly and she cried,*

High Priestess:

> *I have known love's pain.*

Narrator:

> *And Death raised her from the dust saying:*
> *Blessed Be.*
> *And he gave her the Five-Fold Kiss saying,*

High Priest:

> *Only thus shalt thou reach*
> *Joy and Wisdom.*

As he says these words, he unties the cords that bind her.

Narrator:

> *And he taught her all the mysteries*
> *And gave her the necklace*
> *That symbolizes the Circle of reincarnation.*

The High Priest takes the High Priestess' amber and jet necklace from the altar and places it around her neck. The High Priestess picks up the horned crown and the sword from the floor and gives them to the High Priest. They stand next to each other before the altar, he in the position of the Great God, feet together, hands crossed over his chest; and she in the position of the Great Goddess, feet and arms wide open forming a pentagram, which is why she is known as the Star Goddess.

Narrator:

And she instructed him in the mysteries of the holy chalice,
Which is the cauldron of reincarnation. They loved each other
And they were one;
For there are three great mysteries in a man's life.
Magic (love) controls them all.
To achieve love, thou must return
At the same time and the same place
As thy beloved.
And thou must meet again and learn and remember
And love as in the past.
But ere thou art reborn
Thou must die
And prepare thyself for a new body.
And to die, thou must be born.
And without love
A rebirth is impossible.
And our Goddess always inclines herself
Towards joy and love
And loves her children hidden in this life.
And in death she teaches us
How to obtain communion.
And in the world she teaches us

The mystery of the Magic Circle
Which is placed between the worlds.

The High Priestess and High Priest place the scourge, the sword, the crowns, and all the magical implements upon the altar. After this dramatization of the gods' story, the Witch receives the Third Degree Initiation and is declared a High Priest or High Priestess with the right to start his or her own coven.

After this initiation, the Great Rite is conducted in those covens who practice it. The Great Rite is done in private, between the Witches who are married and their spouses, and who desire to achieve a total identification with the Great God and the Great Goddess.

Self Initiation

Many persons who are attracted by Wicca's practices and its laws, but who do not wish to be part of a coven, may initiate themselves into the religion. This may be done by following closely the details of the main ceremony of Wicca and its initiations.

WICCA'S ALPHABET
AND THE MAGICAL IMPLEMENTS

The Wicca alphabet is known as the Theban script or the Wiccan Runes. In ancient times it was used by Witches who wished to exchange messages. In modern times it is used in spells, to write the Witch's name in the Book of Shadows, and sometimes for communication between Witches when the message requires total privacy. As you can see in the illustration, the Runes include several "letters of confusion" that were used in ancient times in the middle of a message to confuse the curious (see figures on page 77).

Among the magical weapons or implements used by the Witches are, as we have seen, the athame or black-handled knife, the bolline or white-handled knife, the magic wand, the pentacle, the ritual scourge, the chalice, the bell, the cords, the censer, the High Priestess' jewels and her crown, the High Priest's crown, and the altar.

The Athame

This is the most important implement used by the Witch. It is used to cast the Circle and during all the ceremonies. The High Priestess and High Priest use the athame to confer the three initiation and to invoke the Lords of the Watch Towers, every Witch receives the athame during the First Degree Initiation and must always bring it with him into the Circle. When the athame is not being used it is placed upon the altar. The athame's handle is inscribed with the main symbols of Wicca as you can see in the accompanying illustrations (see page 77). Among the symbols which are inscribed in the upper part of the handle is the cosmic wheel that represents the eight paths of Wicca. These paths are associated with the eight major Sabbaths or festivals. The magic arrow and the perfect couple (Aradia and Karnayna) are the other symbols found on the upper part of the handle.

The lower part of the athame is inscribed with the symbol of the Great God with his horned crown and the letter "K," which is Karnayna's initial. In the middle of the handle are the symbols of the scourge and Wicca's ritual kiss. At the end of the handle are inscribed the symbols of the waxing and waning Moons (Aradia) and the Hebrew letter Aleph, which represents the "A" of Aradia.

The Magic Sword

The magic sword has the same uses as the athame and is a symbol of great power used by the Witch to invoke and control spirits. The magic sword has the same inscriptions as the athame. It is often used during initiations, especially that of the Third Degree, when it is wielded by the High Priest in his representation of the Great God.

Symbols Inscribed on the Athame and the Magic Sword

Upper Part of the Handle

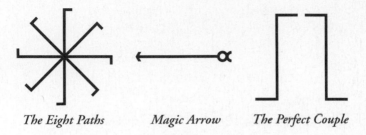

The Eight Paths   Magic Arrow   The Perfect Couple

Lower Part of the Handle

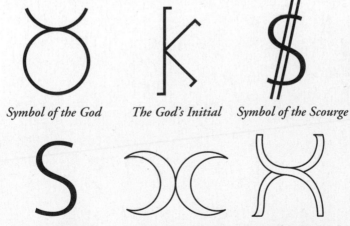

Symbol of the God   The God's Initial   Symbol of the Scourge

Symbol of the Kiss   Symbol of the Goddess   The Goddess' Initial

The Bolline

The bolline is the white-handled knife used by the Witch to inscribe candles and other magical implements. It is also used in many spells. It may never be used outside the Circle. The bolline is inscribed, not only on the upper and lower parts of the handle, but also on the blade.

Symbols Inscribed on the Bolline

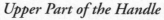

Upper Part of the Handle

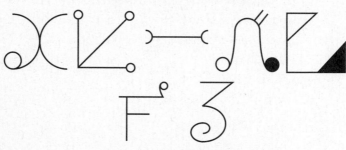

Lower Part of the Handle

CAM

1471 Springfield
back basement suite

black K

back

Upper Part of the Blade

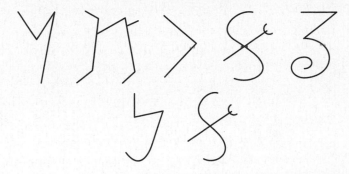

Many Witches used the bolline to inscribe the symbols on the athame and the magic sword. Others use silver ink to draw the symbols on these magical implements. The symbols inscribed on the bolline are very ancient runes and their meaning is not clear.

The Magic Wand

The magic wand may be made of several types of trees but the Witch must go to a forest or park and cut it off the branch of a tree. The trees preferred by Witches to make the magic wand are the oak, the hazel, and the willow.

The magic wand must have the same length as the distance from the elbow to the tip of the middle finger of its owner. It should be about an inch thick and be as straight as possible.

When the Witch has obtained the branch from the adequate tree, he uses the bolline to cut off all the knots on its surface. He then polishes it with sandpaper and with the tip of the bolline makes a hole on one end of the branch. The hole must be about two inches deep. He then pricks his finger with a new needle, lets a few drops of blood fall on a small piece of cotton, and stuffs the cotton inside the hole in the branch. The hole is then sealed with the wax of a white candle in which a pentagram has been inscribed with the bolline. The wand is then painted black and inscribed with a pentagram. Some Witches inscribe their magic names in runes on the wand with the bolline or draw them on it with silver ink. Often the tip of the wand where the blood has been placed is painted in silver, as that is the side of the wand that will be used in all magical work.

After the wand is prepared it must be consecrated with the four elements. To do this the Witch places it over salt (Earth element), passes it over the flame of a candle (Fire element), sprinkles it with water (Water element) and passes it over smoking incense (Air element). He then anoints it with consecrated oil and wine, and blows on it three time in the name of Aradia and Karnayna.

The magic wand is used to invoke and control certain spirits, generally beneficent, who cannot be invoked with the athame or the magic sword. It is also used to gather cosmic energies when the Witch is conducting certain types of magic rituals.

The Pentacle

The pentacle is a round, thin piece of copper, silver, or wood, about seven inches in diameter. It represents the Earth element and may be used to invoke the spirits of this element. Several of the Wiccan symbols are inscribed on the pentacle with the bolline. These symbols can be seen in the next illustration, and include the pentagram or five-pointed star and two triangles, one looking up and the other looking down, representing the Fire and Water elements, respectively. An inverted pentagram is inscribed on the right side of the pentacle and Aradia's and Karnayna's symbols are inscribed on the bottom. The symbols for the kiss and the scourge are beneath them.

The pentacle is also used to place the salt used in the purification of the Circle. Salt is a symbol of the Earth element in the practice of magic and is considered a substance of great purifying powers. The Catholic Church also believes

Wicca's Magical Pentacle

salt to be a purifying element and for this reason it is used during baptismal ceremonies.

The Scourge

The scourge's handle is usually made of birch and painted black. Hanging from the handle are four long strips of thin leather or black silk with a knot at each end. The length of the strips is about twelve inches. The handle is inscribed with the symbols of the various initiations received by its owner. If only the First Degree Initiation has been received the symbol inscribed on the handle is an inverted triangle. When the Second Degree Initiation has been received, its symbol—a pentagram—is added. These are followed by a pentagram topped by an upright triangle when the Third Degree Initiation is received. These symbols may be seen in the accompanying illustration.

First Degree   *Second Degree*   *Third Degree*

Symbols Inscribed on the Scourge's Handle

The scourge is a symbol of power and control. It is used as an instrument of punishment and purification, as Wicca teaches that all magical knowledge must be acquired through suffering. The High Priest and High Priestess, who use the scourge most commonly during rituals, are always gentle in their use of this implement and those who receive the ritual lashings are never hurt. The lashings are symbols of obedience and purification.

The Chalice

The chalice is usually large, as all the members of the coven drink from the wine poured in this ritualistic cup. The chalice may be made of metal or crystal. Some covens have beautiful silver chalices engraved with Celtic symbols, which are the roots of Wicca. It is possible to buy ready-made silver, black, or dark blue chalices already engraved with Wicca's symbol, which is a half moon with a pentagram in the middle. These chalices are generally inexpensive and are easily available in New Age stores. But it is also possible to buy a plain silver cup and draw Wicca's symbol on it with black ink or inscribe it with the bolline. During Wicca's ceremonies the only chalice that lies on the altar is that of the High Priestess who leads the coven. All the other members also have chalices but these are kept on their personal altars.

The chalice is used in every Wiccan ceremony and represents the feminine principle, while the athame represents the male principle. When the High Priestess buries the athame in the chalice of wine presented to her by the High Priest, she is imitating the union between these two principles.

The ritual wine used in Wicca is always sweet wine and symbolizes passion, life, and love. No Wiccan ceremony is complete without the wine, from which all Witches must drink as a symbol of the coven's brotherhood. The first to drink from the chalice is the High Priestess and she must also finish the wine that remains in the cup after all the other Witches have partaken from it.

Symbol Inscribed on the Chalice

The Censer

The censer is of great importance in the Wiccan ceremony because it is a purifying element whose fragrance is used to sweeten and soften the spirits invoked during each ritual. The incenses used always depend on the entities invoked. In simple ceremonies, like the Esbats, frankincense and myrrh are most commonly used. Some modern covens use incense sticks in their rituals, but the more traditional practitioners frown upon this practice as they consider the censer an intrinsic part of the religion.

During the great Sabbaths or when elementals or planetary spirits are invoked, the incenses used are those made of the herbs and fragrances associated with the planets or the four elements. This is of primordial importance in all invocations. If the aroma used in the censer does not correspond to the entity invoked the spirit cannot be contacted. In the second part of this book we will discuss the various herbs and fragrances attributed to the planets and the elements.

The censer used in Wicca is always large, similar to the ones used in most churches. It is also inscribed with the pentagram and half moon, which are Wicca's traditional symbols.

The Bell

The bell is used in all Wiccan ceremonies to mark certain important points in the ritual or to indicate that something has ended or is about to begin. The High Priestess always rings the bell by tapping it lightly with the athame's blade. This ensures that the bell will only ring once each time she taps it. Like other Wiccan implements, the bell is also inscribed with the pentagram and half moon.

The bell may be made of metal or crystal, but most covens prefer metal to avoid accidents where the bell may fall and break.

The Cords

Some of the most powerful and popular spells used by Witches are made with the magic cords. Every First Degree

Witch must have his or her initiation cords, white, red and blue. Of these, the one must commonly used is the blue cord.

When he receives the Second Degree Initiation the Witch already knows how to work with the colors of the four elements: red (Fire element), blue (Air element), green (Water element), and yellow (Earth element). These are the colors used in Wicca to define the four elements and are different than the four traditional colors used in the practice of High Magic. The four traditional colors of the elements are: red (Fire), blue (Water), yellow (Air), and green (Earth). As we can see, these colors are different than those used in Wicca. In the practice of magic the colors and attributes corresponding to the system used are always observed. If the system used is traditional elemental magic, the colors used are the traditional colors of the elements. If the system used is Wicca, the colors used are those of that religion.

The cord used to take the measurements of the Witch in the First Degree Initiation is often worn by that Witch around his waist. At one end of the cord he forms a small circle and unravels a few inches of the cord at the other end. The circle represents the feminine principle, while the frayed end represents the male principle. When he ties the cord around his waist, the Witch passes the frayed end through the Circle to symbolize the union of the male and feminine principles. He then adjusts and ties the cord around his waist. This cord is usually nine feet in length and one of its traditional uses is to measure the diameter of the Magic Circle, which is supposed to measure nine feet. The initiation cord has great powers and it is believed to protect the Witch inside the Circle.

The color cords are used within the Circle when the Witches work their spells as a group. Each cord is used for a specific type of magic. The red cord is used to acquire or control power. The green cord is used for magic spells, as green is the color associated with Venus, the planet of love. The yellow cord is used to obtain money, or for health or business purposes. The blue cord is used to attain happiness, triumphs, joy, and harmony. This color is also used to dispel evil gossip and the destructive intentions of enemies. White is used to acquire peace and balance.

Each Witch decides what he or she wants to acquire through the cords before the coven begins its magic work. After the major ceremony has ended and they have raised the Cone of Power, all the Witches sit on the floor forming a circle. All the chosen cords are tied together at one end and each Witch holds his cord tightly in his hand, keeping a close eye on it. Then they all pull hard on their individual cords until they form a wheel where each cord resembles one of the wheel's spokes. Each person must make sure the cord is taut and must never let it go slack; otherwise, the wheel of cords loses power and balance.

As he holds his cord tightly in his hand, the Witch concentrates on what he wishes to obtain, directing the thought through his hand into the cord. When the wish is strongly visualized in his mind, he rapidly makes a knot on the cord, always keeping it tense. All the time he is visualizing and expressing his desire mentally, the Witch keeps his eyes focused on the center of the cord wheel where all the cords are tied together. This center is the core of the energies of the Cone of Power. Once he has made the knot, he concentrates on another wish and makes another knot. Witches do not ask too many things during their work with cord magic. They prefer to concentrate on one or two things so that the energy will not be dispersed and they may be sure that they will obtain what they wished for.

When they have all made their petitions and tied the knots on the cords, the cord wheel is undone and the cords are untied. Each Witch puts away his or her cord with the knots intact until the next cord session. The knots are not untied until the wish is accomplished.

One of the most famous of the cord spells is the Witch's Ladder. This magic is done with a green cord where forty knots have been tied. These represent the forty traditional lashes that a Witch receives during his or her initiations. The cord is used to contact the unconscious. The Ladder is used at night, just before the Witch goes to sleep. He holds the Ladder in his hands and repeats one single wish on each knot. If he should wake up during the night, he repeats the process until he falls asleep again.

The reason why the Ladder is used immediately before sleep is that when a person is drowsy he falls into the alpha state when it is easier to contact the unconscious. The Witch believes that the unconscious is like a sleeping giant who can get him anything he may wish if he can only contact it and let it know his desires. The persistent use of the Ladder every night asking the same wish ensures that the desire is fulfilled. The Witches never ask anything new through the Ladder until the initial wish is accomplished.

The Witch's Ladder may be used in this manner for self-healing purposes, to get a job, money, love, and anything the Witch may desire, including the control over enemies. The

Witch's Ladder may also be used inside the Magic Circle, when the coven is doing their cord magic. To do this the Witch makes forty knots in a cord concentrating on only one wish. He then uses the Ladder each night to reinforce the petition. When the wish is obtained, the knots are untied and the Ladder is formed again with a new wish.

The Witch's Ladder may be made of different colors, depending on what the Witch desires to accomplish. Green is used for all petitions. Violet, for example, is the most exalted color, associated with the spirit, and used to acquire spiritual evolution.

The Garter

All High Priestesses wear a green garter, whose color represents the Water element in Wicca and the feminine principle. Each time one of her Witches receives the Third Degree Initiation and leaves the coven to start his or her own, the High Priestess adds a silver buckle to her garter, which she always wears on her left thigh. The High Priestess is considered the origin and mother of every coven that is born of her, and the more buckles she has on her garter, the greater her power and prestige. This is one of the oldest traditions of Wicca and dates from the times of the Celts.

The Crown

The High Priestess wears a crown around her forehead that is more like a diadem. It is usually made of silver with a half moon on the middle. The half moon always points upwards and is a symbol of Aradia.

The High Priest wears a crown topped with antlers representing Karnayna. The High Priest only uses this crown during the Third Degree Initiations.

The Necklace

The ritualistic necklace of the female Witch, especially the High Priestess, who always wears it, is made of alternating amber and jet beads. The beads represent the power of the Great Goddess on earth.

Other Jewels

Witches are very fond of ritualistic jewelry. One of the most popular magical symbols used is the Egyptian ankh, which is made of a cross topped with a circle. This was the symbol of life among Egyptians and all the statues of their gods carried it in their hands. In Wicca, the ankh is a symbol of the goddess Isis, who is associated with the moon and is one of the names of the Great Goddess. Both men and women wear the ankh either in necklaces or rings.

Silver rings with the various stones associated with the planets and the elements are also commonly used, as well as necklaces made of natural amulets. The pentagram and half moon, Wicca's traditional symbol, is also worn in rings, bracelets, and necklaces.

Some Witches wear seven rings, representing the seven traditional planets: Sun, Moon, Mars, Mercury, Jupiter, Venus, and Saturn. The rings are made of the metals and stones attributed to each of the planets.

One of the most spectacular rings used by many Witches is made of silver and the front is shaped like an eagle's claw that holds a crystal ball, a symbol of the moon. This crystal ball is fairly large and may be used to look into the future. Crystal balls are sometimes used within the Circle to "scry," or to obtain visions of the future. To do this one of the Witches sits on the floor facing the east. A white candle is placed on each side of the crystal ball. The Witch visualizes the past behind him and the future in front of him. The rest of the coven close their eyes and concentrate on the crystal ball. The Witch gazes at the ball while keeping his mind free of thoughts. As a flow of images begin to stream into his mind, he describes them in a slow and measured voice. One of the Witches, who always acts as a scribe, writes the visions in a special notebook where the date of the scrying session is also written.

During each scrying session a different member of the coven looks into the crystal ball. This gives everyone the opportunity to develop the power of clairvoyance. The favorite crystal ball is made of white quartz, which is not always completely transparent as white quartz is often filled with inclusions. These balls are generally very expensive, and the larger and more transparent balls can have exorbitant prices.

Every object made of white quartz, including the crystal ball, must be cleansed and purified beforehand by placing it in saltwater for twenty-four hours and later rinsed and exposed to the Sun for at least six hours.

The Altar

The Wiccan altar is only a symbol to the Witch, who rarely works upon it. It is mostly used to place the magical implements when they are not in use and the two white candles that rest on each end.

The altar is usually covered with a piece of black cloth that reaches to the floor. The cloth is nearly always velvet or satin.

As the altar is a symbol of the Earth element, it is always placed on the north of the Circle, which corresponds to this element. Witches generally conduct their magic facing the north quarter.

Many of the ritualistic actions of the High Priestess or High Priest are conducted facing the altar or behind it, but it is never used as a central focus of the ceremonies. It is one of the most important magical implements of Wicca and it is indispensable for the coven's work, but its symbolism is more spiritual than material. Although all the ritualistic actions of the ceremonies take place before or behind the altar, it is never in the middle of the Circle and is not the place where the Witches raise the Cone of Power.

All the rituals, initiations, magical practices, and spells, and the use of herbs, oils, and incenses are handwritten in a mysterious volume known as the Book of Shadows. In the Part Two of this book, we will discuss in some depth the magic of the Witches as described in the Book of Shadows.

PART TWO

THE BOOK OF
SHADOWS
(THE MAGIC OF WITCHES)

THE BOOK OF SHADOWS

The Book of Shadows is the journal wherein Witches write down all their ceremonies, the initiations, the days where Esbats and Sabbaths are observed, and all the spells used in the religion. Herbs, incenses, oils, magic perfumes, information on the elements, the planets, planetary hours, colors, elementals, familiars, invocations, evocations, and other important rituals are also included in this book, which is handwritten and copied by each Witch from the High Priestess' own Book of Shadows. In this section we will discuss much of the information that appears in this book.

Familiars

A familiar is an animal used by a Witch during rituals and spell casting. In ancient times it was believed that a Witch could send his familiar to an enemy with precise instructions to harm that person. In modern times not every Witch has a familiar and the ones who have these entities rarely use them during rituals. It is believed that the animal used as a familiar adds its energies to the magic performed by the Witch to give it more power.

The best known familiar is the black cat and one of the magic rituals used by Witches with this animal is to rub its pelt with salt at the stroke of midnight to acquire money. Other common familiars include owls, ravens, and dogs. For some reason, frogs are sometimes associated with Wicca, but only in Black Magic practices.

The *totem* is a familiar that protects a Witch or a magician. This is the animal most commonly identified with that person. Many magical systems teach that every human being has a totem. This concept originates with the shamans of some of Native American tribes. Usually this is an animal with whom the person tends to identify. For example, someone who loves doves and feels strangely drawn to them may possibly have a dove as his or her totem. The totem is a spiritual entity and everything that is connected with it is very beneficial to the person with whom it is associated. It is possible, in certain moments, that the totem may actually materialize before a person to let him or her know that it is near and will always protect him or her. For example, I love wolves, with whom I feel a great affinity. On the door to my office I have a beautiful mandala with a wolf in the middle. One afternoon, minutes before leaving the office, I was admiring the mandala and feeling a deep affection towards the wolf. Shortly afterwards I left the office and went to the garage where I usually leave my car. Suddenly, I saw the wolf of the mandala emerge from one of the corners of the garage and come running towards me. It was a beautiful animal of huge proportions, but I felt no fear.

As soon as it reached my side, it began to lick my hands. Within minutes a man came out of a minivan and ran to me. "Be careful," he said. "This is a wild wolf. I have tamed it but it is still a wild creature. It could attack you."

"Don't worry," I said. "It would never do me any harm." For a few moments I leaned over the wolf who put its paws on my shoulders and began to lick my face. "I can't believe it," said its owner. "It has never shown me such affection." "It's because we are old friends," I said, to the man's surprise. "We've known each other for a very long time."

A few moments later I left the garage and I never saw the wolf or its owner again. But it was an unforgettable moment, a "synchronized" event, where the wolf of the mandala wanted to let me know that it shared my feelings and that it would always protect me. I protect it also because the wolf is one of the animals on the endangered list and I have always been very active with organizations that protect the wolf and other endangered species. It is of great help to any individual to know who is his or her totem. Once you know who is your protective animal, you should keep images of it around the house or office or carry amulets representing it for good luck and protection.

ELEMENTALS

The elementals are entities usually associated with the four elements. Fairies, elves, and sylphs are creatures with iridescent wings similar to those of butterflies; they belong to the Air element. They are used in many types of magic and the best day to invoke them is at midnight on Midsummer, which is observed on the eve of June 24. This is one of the most magical nights of the year and it is said that spells cast on this night are very effective.

Undines are described as very beautiful creatures. They are said to be translucent, of a blue-gray color, and belong to the Water element. Undines are usually invoked in love magic, as love is associated with this element.

Salamanders belong to the Fire element. They are said to be made of fire, and resemble tiny flaming dragons. They are used in power spells.

Gnomes belong to the Earth element. They are visualized as bearded, and about two feet tall. Gnomes are said to reside in the depths of the Earth and to be accomplished miners. All the metals, especially gold, precious stones, and the hidden treasures of the Earth belong to them. They are invoked in money spells.

Witches use another type of elemental which they create themselves from their own energies. These elementals are sent by the Witch to carry out his or her wishes. One of the ways used by the Witch to create an elemental is to rub the hands together very rapidly and then holding the palms facing each other, about eight inches apart. A large ball of energy is visualized between the palms, which are moved backwards and forwards several times to increase the energy. Through the power of imagination the ball of energy is given a specific form and given a name. As the hands are moved back and forth, the Witch charges the elemental with a special desire or purpose. Then, with a powerful thrust of will power, he sends the elemental to carry out that desire or purpose. If what the Witch wants to do is to send a special message to another person, the elemental rushes through space and delivers the intended message, which the other person perceives as his or her spontaneous thought. The person then acts immediately upon this "thought," exactly as the Witch intended.

Elementals are often used when the Witch wants a specific amount of money. The elemental transforms the energies it finds on its path into money opportunities for its creator.

Once the elemental has fulfilled the Witch's commands, it is called back to its owner who reabsorbs its energies, as it is dangerous to leave the elemental floating freely in space.

The late Alex Sanders was a very famous Witch and High Priest, known in England as "the King of the Witches." He had a coven in London which he directed with his wife Maxine, who acted as his High Priestess. There are several books written about his life and he left a series of lectures that are among the best known writings about Wicca.

I met Alex Sanders when I was still working for the United Nations in Vienna. Alex had an elemental, created as I have already described, which he named Michael and which he often used for different purposes. During a reunion with him and his coven in a London pub, Alex told me the following story. One night, just before celebrating one of their Esbats, Alex and his coven went to a pub as was usually their custom before their rituals. One of the women in the coven had many warts on her face, a misfortune she had inherited from her grandmother. As soon as the coven entered the pub, one of the waiters began to tease the woman, making fun of her warts. The coven tried nicely to dissuade the waiter from continuing his cruel jokes, but he continued teasing the woman until she broke down and began to cry, overcome with shame and humiliation. One of the male members of the coven stood up angrily, with the intention of striking the waiter, but Alex held him back. "Leave this in my hands," he said. He turned to the waiter and said, "You shouldn't be making fun of her because you seem to be sprouting a few warts yourself." The waiter laughed and told Alex he was crazy. A few moments later, the coven arose from the table and left the pub.

The next day Alex called his elemental Michael, charged it with special instructions, and sent it to the waiter. Several weeks later the coven returned to the pub. The woman who had been teased by the waiter had lost all her warts. These had been transferred by Michael to the waiter, who now had three times as many warts on his face. None of the members of the coven made fun of the waiter or made any comments about his warts. But as soon as he saw them come in and noticed the woman with her face cleared of warts, he ran away from the pub, where he never showed up again. This happened in the same pub where Alex told me the story.

Witches do not always use their powers to harm an enemy, but as we discussed earlier, the Law of Three forces them to return either good or evil three times as strong.

The power of the elementals is very real and is used often by many Witches, but it is a dangerous power because an uncontrolled elemental force can be devastating to the person who creates it. For that reason, it is not advisable for inexperienced persons carry out experiments with elementals unless they know how to control them.

HERBS

Herbs are of great importance in the practice of Wicca and are used in healings, in magic baths, and in all kinds of spells. Witches classify herbs according to their powers and the elements that ruled them.

The following is a list of the herbs, trees, leaves, flowers, fruits, and roots that are most popular among Witches, the planets and elements to which they belong, and their most common uses.

Herb	Planet(s)	Element	Uses
Adam and Eve	Venus	Water	Love, union, marriage, joy
Almond	Mercury	Air	Money, prosperity
Artemisa	Venus	Earth	Purification, exorcisms, psychic abilities

Herb	Planet(s)	Element	Uses
Asafetida	Mars	Fire	Exorcisms, purification, protection
Balm of Gilead	Venus	Water	Health, cleansings, love
Barley	Venus	Earth	Money, love, fertility
Banana	Venus	Water	Love, prosperity, fertility
Basil	Mars	Fire	Love, cleansings, prosperity
Beet	Saturn	Earth	Forbidden love, unfaithful lovers
Betony	Jupiter	Fire	Protection, purification, love
Blackberry	Venus	Water	Health, money, protection
Buckthorn	Saturn	Water	Ward off evil, exorcisms, court cases

Herb	Planet(s)	Element	Uses
Cabbage	Moon	Water	Love, money, prosperity
Cardamon	Venus	Water	Love, money
Carnation	Sun	Fire	Love, Protection
Carrot	Mars	Earth	Fertility, money, virility, love
Cascara sagrada	Jupiter	Earth	Court cases, cleansings, money
Cedar	Sun	Fire	Power, energy, money, health
Chamomile	Sun	Fire	Love, money, health
Cherry	Venus	Water	love, evolution
Chicory	Sun	Air	Cleansings, good luck, invisibility
Chili	Mars	Fire	Love, to destroy spells
Chrysanthemum	Sun	Fire	Cleansings, money, alcohol

Herb	Planet(s)	Element	Uses
Cinnamon	Sun	Fire	Love, success, money
Clover	Mercury	Air	Luck, money, protection, triumph
Coconut	Moon	Water	Cleansings, protection, purification
Corn	Sun, Venus	Earth	Love, money, protection, prosperity
Cucumber	Moon	Water	Health, fertility, chastity
Cumin	Sun, Mars	Fire	Protection, money, fidelity
Cypress	Saturn	Earth	Longevity, health, protection
Damiana	Mars	Fire	Love, meditation, psychic abilities
Date	Sun	Air	Impotence, fertility, money

Herb	*Planet(s)*	*Element*	*Uses*
Elder	Venus	Water	Cleansings, health, protection
Elm	Saturn	Water	Love, power, fertility
Elm	Mercury, Saturn	Air	Cleansings, against robberies
Eucalyptus	Moon	Water	Health, cleansings
Fern	Mercury	Air	Health, love, prophetic dreams, cleansings
Gardenia	Venus, Moon	Water	Love, peace, health, meditation
Garlic	Mars	Fire	Protection, cleansings, passion
Geranium	Venus	Water	Love, health, protection
Ginger	Mars	Fire	Love, power, control, protection, triumphs

Herb	Planet(s)	Element	Uses
Ginseng	Sun	Fire	Energy, health, love
Grape	Moon, Venus	Water	Fertility, mental power, money
Guinea Pepper	Mars	Fire	Power, triumph, to speed up spells
Hazel	Sun	Air	Protection, good luck, joy
Hyssop	Jupiter	Fire	Purification, cleansings, protection
Iris	Moon, Venus	Water	Purification, wisdom, psychic abilities
Jasmine	Moon, Venus	Water	Love, money, prophetic dreams
John the Conqueror	Mars	Fire	Love, money, control

Herb	Planet(s)	Element	Uses
Laurel	Sun	Fire	Money, power, triumphs, psychic abilities
Lavender	Mercury	Air	Love, protection, health
Lemon	Moon, Venus	Water	Love, cleansings, longevity
Lettuce	Venus	Water	Purity, money, love, protection
Lily	Moon, Venus	Water	Purity, peace, destroy love spells
Linden	Jupiter	Air	Love, luck, protection, longevity
Mandrake	Mercury	Fire	Love, money, power, health
Mallow	Moon	Water	Love, protection, cleansings

Herb	Planet(s)	Element	Uses
Marjoram	Mercury	Air	Protection, cleansings, luck
Mint	Mercury	Fire	Mental power, love, health, cleansings
Mistletoe	Sun, Venus	Air	Love, protection, fertility, cleansings
Myrtle	Venus	Water	Love, fertility, peace, money
Mulberry	Mercury	Air	Strength, peace, cleansings
Mullein	Saturn	Fire	Courage, protection, health, exorcisms
Oak	Sun	Fire	Health, power, money, luck, virility
Oats	Venus	Earth	Money, abundance

Herb	Planet(s)	Element	Uses
Onion	Mars	Fire	Love, money, protection, alcoholism
Orange	Sun, Venus	Fire	Love, money, health, abundance
Orchid	Venus	Air	Love, peace, harmony, prosperity
Papaya	Moon	Water	Love, protection, money
Paprika	Mars	Fire	Control over enemies, triumph, love
Parsley	Mercury	Air	Passion, money, purification
Pear	Moon, Venus	Water	Love, abundance, court cases
Pennyroyal	Mars	Fire	Evolution, cleansings
Peony	Sun	Fire	Luck, money, cleansings

Herb	Planet(s)	Element	Uses
Pepper	Mars	Fire	Power, money, cleansings
Pine	Mars	Air	Power, triumph, money, health, cleansings
Pineapple	Sun	Fire	Luck, money, health
Plum	Moon, Venus	Water	Love, psychic abilities
Pomegranate	Mercury	Fire	Cleansings, fertility, love, health, money
Potato	Moon	Earth	Money, health, exorcisms
Pumpkin	Moon, Venus	Water	Love, money, abundance
Purslane	Moon	Water	Love, luck, protection, joy
Rice	Sun	Air	Fertility, money

Herb	Planet(s)	Element	Uses
Rose	Venus	Water	Love, health, power, luck, protection
Rosemary	Sun	Fire	Love, passion, money, health
MenRue	Mars	Fire	Exorcisms, health, mental power, love
Saffron	Sun, Venus	Water	Love, prosperity
Sage	Jupiter	Air	Health, protection, cleansings, longevity
Sarsaparrilla	Jupiter	Fire	Love, money, cleansings
Seaweed	Moon	Water	Cleansings, sea spells, psychic abilities
Senna	Mercury	Air	Love, fertility
Spearmint	Mercury, Moon	Air	Health, love, money, cleansings

Herb	Planet(s)	Element	Uses
Spurge	Mars	Fire	Cleansings, power, exorcisms
Strawberry	Venus	Water	Love, health, prosperity
Sunflower	Sun	Fire	Love, health, fertility, money
Tobacco	Mars	Fire	Health, power, triumph
Tonka bean	Venus	Earth	Love, money, triumph
Tulip	Venus	Earth	Love, protection, money
Valerian	Venus	Water	Love, cleansings, prophetic dreams
Vanilla	Venus	Water	Love, luck, mental power
Vervain	Venus	Water	Love, money, protection, luck, peace

Herb	Planet(s)	Element	Uses
Violet	Venus	Earth	Love, peace, protection, luck, psychic abilities
Walnut	Sun	Fire	Health, mental power, fertility
Wheat	Sun, Venus	Air	Money, fertility
Willow	Moon, Venus	Water	Love, protection, health
Yam	Sun, Venus	Earth	love, money, good luck
Yerba mate	Sun	Fire	Cleansings, love, exorcisms, fidelity
Yohimbe	Venus	Earth	Love, seduction
Yucca	Mars	Fire	Purification, exorcisms, peace, psychic abilities

The reader may notice that the planet that rules an herb is not necessarily associated with its own element. For example, some of the herbs under the sun's rulership do not belong to the Fire element, which is the sun's natural element. This can be seen throughout the list.

Later on, in the spell section, we will discuss various magic spells used by Witches with some of these herbs.

Warning: Some plants, like saffron, plum leaves, Balm of Gilead, cypress leaves and others may be poisonous or fatal if they are ingested, if they come in contact with open wounds, or if they are inhaled when used as incense. Pay heed to this warning when using these plants. The sale and use of some of the plants listed may be restricted by state laws and even the possession of some of them may be dangerous. It is wise to verify the nature of any plant that is used on the body with a book on herbs and their uses.

COLORS

As we have seen, Witches use colors continuously in their magical practices. There are seven basic colors in the solar spectrum: red, orange, yellow, green, blue, indigo, and violet. These are the same colors that may be seen in the rainbow as it is formed by the refraction or division of light. All of these colors are hidden in each light ray and in white. Black is the absence of light and color.

In reality, there are only three primary colors: red, yellow, and blue. All the colors we know are formed from a mixture of these three. Some hues include a tinge of white or black. If we look closely at the solar spectrum, we will see that orange, which follows red, is a combination of red and yellow, which follows orange in the spectrum. Green is a combination of yellow and blue. Violet is a combination of red and indigo because the two ends of the spectrum join at the end.

Colors are associated with the planets, the zodiac signs and the elements. Yellow is associated with the Air element, red with Fire, blue with Water, and green with Earth. Zodiac signs also have their own colors:

Aries	red
Taurus	green
Gemini	orange
Cancer	light blue/silver
Leo	yellow/gold
Virgo	blue-gray/brown
Libra	blue/pink
Scorpio	dark red
Sagittarius	indigo
Capricorn	black
Aquarius	violet
Pisces	aqua blue

The colors of the planets are as follows:

Sun	yellow/gold (Leo)
Moon	silver/violet (Cancer)
Mars	red (Aries, Scorpio)
Venus	green (Taurus, Libra)
Mercury	orange (Gemini, Virgo)
Jupiter	indigo (Sagittarius)
Saturn	black (Saturn)
Neptune	aqua blue (Pisces)
Uranus	violet (Aquarius)
Pluto	dark red (Scorpio)

As may be seen from the preceding lists, the colors of the planets correspond, in the most part, with those of the signs they rule.

Witches also use the colors to make small sachet bags for protection and for good luck; to invoke elemental or planetary spirits; in their cord magic, and for healing. To make a sachet bag for protection they generally use the color of their birth signs. If they want to attract love, they use green, the color of Venus; if they want money, they use yellow or blue, which are the respective colors of the Sun and Jupiter, the planets associated with money and prosperity. The sachet bags are filled with herbs, stones, and other natural amulets associated with whatever the Witch wishes to attract to himself.

To invoke elemental or planetary spirits the colors used are those associated with the proper element or planet, as we have seen.

Healings through colors is known as *chromotherapy*; *chromo* meaning "color" in Greek. Following is a list of the colors of the solar spectrum and the illnesses they are said to heal.

Red: this is a dynamic and stimulating color, used to heal blood-related diseases such as anemia, problems with the liver and blood circulation, and to give added strength to a weak person.

Orange: it is used often to heal respiratory illnesses such as asthma and bronchitis, and to combat depression.

Yellow: it acts as a sedative and is excellent for stomach ailments and digestive complaints. It is also used to alleviate constipation and menstruation disorders. It eases fear and strengthens the mind.

Green: this is the most commonly used color in chromotherapy as it is excellent in many types of healing. It is especially effective in heart ailments, chronic headaches, ulcers, and cancer. It also helps strengthen the immunity system.

Blue: it is especially used to alleviate inflammations, both internal and external. It is excellent to heal burns and wounds. It is also used against rheumatism, arthritis, and muscular pains.

Indigo: it is often used to help heal eye problems, poor vision, and especially cataracts. It also helps to counteract hearing loss and to drive away fears and to alleviate emotional problems.

Violet: it is very effective in the healing of mental imbalance and in bringing harmony to the nervous system. It is also said to help diminish hair loss. It is excellent to help develop psychic powers, such as telepathy, intuition, and clairvoyance. It helps against insomnia and promotes prophetic dreams.

Color healings are used in various forms. One of the easiest and most effective is done by placing a piece of cloth of the appropriate color on the affected area. The cloth is left in place for at least an hour while the person relaxes. In cases of extreme weakness, anemia, or circulatory problems, the cloth must be large enough to cover the person from head to foot.

Color light bulbs are also used. The patient lies down facing upwards and is surrounded with several lit light bulbs of the appropriate color. The room must be in total darkness so that the color rays will vibrate over the person with the greatest intensity possible. The person who undergoes this color light treatment must remain in this position one hour daily. This is one of the most powerful and effective uses of chromotherapy.

Witches also drink juices or liquids of the color associated with an illness they want to heal. The liquid is poured in a bottle painted in the appropriate color, which is then closed tightly and placed by a windowsill for several hours so it may gather solar energies within itself. This is always done during the waxing period of the moon. Sometimes a stone of the same color is affixed to the bottle top for added healing energies. These liquids, charged with the healing color and the power of solar rays, are excellent natural remedies for the healing of many illnesses.

Colored bottles are also used to prepare love philters, to attract money, for energy, and for magnetic power. They are always prepared during the waxing moon, preferably when the planet that rules what is desired is well aspected. For example, one type of love philter is made by boiling red wine with cinnamon, a pinch of vervain, ginger, apple peel, cloves, and honey. The wine is strained and poured into a green bottle, the color of Venus, which is then capped tightly. A rose quartz, associated with love and Venus, is glued to the bottle top. The bottle is placed on a windowsill during the waxing moon and is left there during seven days to gather the solar and lunar energies. After this time, the wine is offered to the person desired. If he or she drinks it, the results are assured. The person who prepares the philter may also drink of it without any untoward effects.

NUMBERS

Witches base all their magic, rituals, and spells on the power of numbers. Some spells are done for a period of three, seven, or nine days; others require more time. The knots made on the Witch's Ladder may be nine or forty, depending on the Witch's purpose. For example, if what he wants is money, he raises the Cone of Power, concentrates firmly on his desire and yells "money!" He then makes a knot with all his strength on the Ladder's cord. As he does this, he is running around the magic circle. When he feels he has accumulated enough energy, he yells "money" again and makes a second knot above the first. He repeats these actions nine times. The next day he places a high denomination bill in front of him and unties one of the knots over the bill, saying:

I've done the spell and done it right
My magic works through day and night
This bill will grow and multiply
By nine and seven magnified.

This is repeated during nine days until all the knots have been untied. The Witch then carries the bill on his person during seven days to complete the spell. The bill, which is the symbol of the multiplied money desired by the Witch, is put away in a safe place or placed upon the altar.

A similar spell with the Ladder may be made for love or anything else the Witch may desire, always using the appropriate numbers. The spell chants, often created by the Witch himself, should always rhyme for added power.

Many of the baths and cleansing used in Wicca also use numbers. Baths for love or money generally use three, five, or seven different herbs. Baths or cleansings for protection or exorcisms use three, seven, or nine herbs.

The zodiac signs and the planets are also ascribed special numbers and are used in the Witch's most powerful spells and rituals.

Following are the numbers ascribed to the zodiac signs:

Aries	9
Taurus	6
Gemini	5
Cancer	2
Leo	1, 4
Virgo	5
Libra	6
Scorpio	9
Sagittarius	3
Capricorn	8
Aquarius	4
Pisces	7

The numbers associated with the planets are:

Sun	6
Moon	9
Mars	5
Mercury	8
Venus	7
Jupiter	4
Saturn	3
Uranus	2
Neptune	1
Pluto	0

Many Witches also use numerology to ensure that the sum total of their magical names is the same as their birth names or that they add up to power numbers like 3, 7, or 9. Some Witches consider thirteen to be a number of great power and others believe it to bring back luck. Modern numerology ascribes the following numbers to the letters of the alphabet. (The numbers used are 1 to 9 and for that reason some letters share the same number.):

a, j, s	1
b, k, t	2
c, l, u	3
d, m, v	4
e, n, w	5
f, o, x	6
g, p, y	7
h, q, z	8
i, r	9

According to this list the name of a person called Ada Smith adds up to 3. This number is obtained by adding the value of each letter in the name.

A – 1
D – 4
A – 1
―――――
        6

S – 1
M – 4
I – 9
T – 2
H – 8
―――――
        24 = 2 + 4 = 6

Ada   = 6
Smith = 6
―――――
        12 = 1 + 2 = 3

The sum total of the name must be reduced to one digit. That is why Smith, which adds up to 24, is reduced to 6; and Ada Smith, which adds up to 12, is reduced to 3.

If Ada Smith wants her magical name to have the same sum total as her given name she chooses a magical name she likes and adds one or more letters until both names add the same. For example, if the magical name she has chosen is Circe, which adds up to 29 (2 + 9 = 11 = 1 + 1 = 2), she will need to add another letter so that the name adds up to 3 as Ada Smith. This letter would be A, whose value is 1 and added to Circe would add up to 3. The A could be added to the end of Circe, making it Circea. Both Circea and Ada Smith add up to 3, making Circea a powerful magical name for Ada Smith.

Some Witches change their names, adopting others that add up to power numbers like 3, 7, 9, or 21. There are double digits like 11, 2, 22, and 33, which are known as master numbers. Both 11 and 22 are considered to be so powerful that only persons with great magical knowledge and power can work with them. These numbers are never reduced to one digit. The reason 21 is considered a master number is that it is really 7 multiplied by 3. The number 33 is associated with the age of Jesus when he died and also with the Law of Three.

The numerical value of the letters is also used in many powerful spells. A common practice among some Witches is to write a wish on a piece of paper and add up the numbers of the letters in the wish, reducing them to one digit. That number is then written daily with magical ink on the palms of the hands and the soles of the feet until the wish is realized. This may be done to attract someone's love, to get money, or for anything else the Witch may desire.

There are several ways to make magical ink. One of them is to dissolve gum arabic and the resin known as dragon's blood in a small quantity of alcohol. This tincture is energized with four elements, passing it over the flame of a red candle to consecrate it in the Fire element; passing it over water to consecrate it with the Water element; over incense to consecrate it in the Air element; and over salt to consecrate it in the Earth element. Many Witches use a white feather, consecrated in the same manner, to write with the magic ink. There are may other ways to use numbers and the numerical values of things to accomplish what is desired.

INCENSES

Incenses are very important in Wicca and other magical practices because of their fragrances and how they affect the mind. Many scientific studies have been conducted on the influence of smells on the human being.

For example, the smell of mint is used in some schools to revitalize their students, as laboratory tests have confirmed that the aroma of mint makes the mind more alert. This is also the reason why most dental pastes use the smell of mint as their most important ingredient, as people feel refreshed and alert after using them. It has also been discovered that the smell of cinnamon induces feelings of warmth and love in some people. For this reason it is considered aphrodisiacal by many neurologists. The smells of vanilla, coffee, and tobacco help many people relax. That is why the use of certain aromas is so common in the practice of magic.

Witches know that odors affect the unconscious mind, helping to release powerful psychic energies during important rituals. Each planet and each element, as well as all spiritual entities, may be contacted through the incenses ascribed to them. As we saw on the section on herbs, these are associated with the planets and the elements. These herbs are often used in planetary and elemental incenses, when burning them in special combinations over lit charcoal. All spiritual entities, both the positive and the negative, are also associated with certain planets and elements. If one knows which planet and element are ascribed to a specific entity, one immediately knows which types of herbs may be used to contact them. For example, the Archangel Raphael rules the Air element, and is associated with both the Sun and Mercury. An appropriate incense to contact Raphael, according to the list of herbs already given, would include elm leaves (Mercury and Air), marjoram (Mercury and Air), parsley (Mercury and Air), wheat (Sun and Air), and bits of dates (Sun and Air). To make the aroma more agreeable one may add one or more of the spices and resins more commonly associated with the elements and planets, as shown in the following list.

Resins and Spices	Planet(s)	Element
Myrrh	Saturn	Earth
Spikenard	Saturn, Mercury	Earth, Air
Patchouli	Saturn	Earth
Cassia	Saturn	Earth
Dragon's blood	Mars	Fire
Mustard	Mars	Fire
Asafetida	Mars	Fire
Galangal	Mars	Fire

Resins and Spices	Planet(s)	Element
Gum Arabic	Sun	Fire
Vanilla	Sun	Fire
Cinnamon	Sun, Venus	Fire, Earth
Frankincense	Sun	Fire
Copal	Sun	Fire
Benzoin	Venus	Earth
Sandalwood	Venus	Earth
Storax	Venus, Mercury	Earth, Air
Vetivert	Venus	Earth
Aniseed	Mercury	Air
Lavender	Mercury	Air
Civet	Venus	Earth
Musk	Venus	Earth
Ambergris	Venus	Earth
Cloves	Mercury	Air
Bergamot	Mercury	Air
Camphor	Moon	Water
Orris root	Moon	Water
Galbanum	Moon	Air
Ylang-Ylang	Moon	Water
Nutmeg	Jupiter	Fire
Olibanum	Jupiter	Fire

For Raphael's incense, one could add lavender and aniseed for the planet Mercury and the Air element; and frankincense and gum arabic for the Sun. This would create an intensely aromatic incense of great magical power.

To invoke lunar entities, including the Great Goddess and the Archangel Gabriel, one would use lunar herbs like eucalyptus, purslane, and willow leaves, adding camphor, ylang-ylang, and orris root. This is a lunar incense of great potency and a powerful aroma.

Each spiritual entity invoked in Wicca or in any High Magic ritual requires the herbs, resins, and spices that attract that spirit according to its planetary and elemental associations. Otherwise the entity may not be contacted.

Many New Age stores carry a great variety of incenses that come in sticks, cones, powder, oils, and perfumes. Many of these incenses, especially the ones that are made of resins or certain fragrances, like cinnamon, rose, jasmine, or frankincense, are used in rituals of lesser importance or to cleanse the place where a ritual is to take place. They are also excellent to dispel negative vibrations in the home. One of the most popular incenses of this type, which is used very often in meditations and cleansings, is Nag Shampa. This incense may be found in cones and sticks and is commonly used in Indian temples and to invoke Hindu deities like Ganesh, Laxshmi, Vishnu, and Shiva. Also very popular are the bunches of dried herbs that are sold already tied and ready to burn. The most common are made of sage, cedar, and lavender. This type of incense originates from the ritualistic practices of Native Americans.

Incenses also come in natural oil form. These are most commonly used in aromatherapy lamps and are steadily growing in popularity. Many persons use the aromatherapy lamps for relaxation and to perfume their homes.

Some of the aromatherapy lamps are electrical but most of them use tea lights. The lamp has a small basin where the liquid incense is placed. Underneath the basin is a small space for the tea light. As the tea light burns it heats the oil incense whose aroma is then dispersed throughout the room. Aromatherapy lamps are highly recommended by many psychologists for the relaxation and well being of persons who suffer from severe forms of stress or insomnia. The most popular fragrances used are sandalwood, lavender, mint, cinnamon, rose, and vanilla. This shows that science has finally discovered the influence that odors have on the mind, something that Witches have known for many centuries.

Following is a list of the most common incenses used by Witches in their rituals and ceremonies. These fragrances are used by themselves or in combination with other ingredients to increase their power. They are burned over one or more pieces of lit charcoal.

Incense	*Uses*
Musk	to attract love and marriage
Asafetida	for exorcisms and to dispel negative vibrations
Benzoin	for purification, prosperity, mental power, and love spells; it is one of the magic ink ingredients
Garlic skin	for purification and to drive away evil spirits
Cinnamon	for love incenses and to attract money

Incense	*Uses*
Cumin	to attract money and prosperity
Gum arabic	for purification and to protect the home; it is one of magic ink ingredients
Bay leaf	for health, triumph, prosperity, and abundance; it is also used to increase mental power
Cedar	for protection, spirituality, and to attract money
Civet	to attract love and marriage
Cloves	for money, protection, love, and purification
Copal	for protection, purification, and spirituality; it is also used to cleanse white quartz and other stones before a ritual
Dragon's blood	for love, protection, triumph, and for control in every situation
Fernit	is burned inside the home to exorcize evil and outside to bring rain
Lavender	for love and prosperity
Frankincense	for protection, purification and to invoke powerful entities
Myrrh	for healing, exorcisms, peace, and during meditations
Olibanum	for money, prosperity, and exorcisms

Incense	*Uses*
Rosemary	for a restful sleep, peace, and good health; it is also recommended to restore youthfulness, attract love, and to increase mental power
Sage	for money, protection, spirituality, and good health
Sandalwood	for love and good luck
Storax	for money, abundance, and prosperity; also used in meditations and to attract powerful spirits
Damiana	to go into trances during meditations
Mandrake	to attract love and good luck
John the Conqueror	for love, money, and triumph
Salpeter	to multiply the effect of other incenses and to attract money in large quantities
Patchouli	for love, money, and good luck
Orris root	to attract love and marriage
Aniseed	for love, money, and good health; it is also used for protection and purification
Valerian	for exorcisms, during meditations and for money

Witches also prepare incense combinations for the various zodiac signs and to achieve specific goals. The following is a list of several of these formulas:

Aries incense: two parts of frankincense, one of ginger, one of paprika, and one of cedar.

Taurus incense: two parts of cinnamon, two of benzoin, and a few drops of rose oil.

Gemini incense: two parts of gum arabic, lemon and orange rinds, and cloves

Cancer incense: two parts of myrrh, one of sandalwood, one of eucalyptus, lemon rind, and a pinch of camphor.

Leo incense: two parts of frankincense, one of bay leaf, one of sandalwood, and one of cinnamon.

Virgo incense: two parts of olibanum, one of patchouli, a pinch of salt, and dried willow leaves.

Libra incense: two parts of sandalwood, one of cinnamon, one of vervain, and a few drops of rose oil.

Scorpio incense: four parts of benzoin, one of olibanum, one of black pepper, one of sandalwood, and one of cedar.

Sagittarius incense: one part of storax, one of cloves, pomegranate rind, and a few drops of ambergris.

Capricorn incense: two parts of sandalwood, one part of benzoin, one of patchouli, and powdered pumice stone.

Aquarius incense: one part of olibanum, one part of cypress leaves, and one of damiana.

Pisces incense: one part of seaweed, one part of myrrh, one of eucalyptus, and lemon rind.

Money incense: two parts of frankincense, one of cinnamon, one of nutmeg, lemon and orange rinds, and one of bay leaf.

Love incense: two parts dragon's blood, one of orris root, one of cinnamon, one of red rose petals, one of patchouli, and one of musk.

Incense for the consecration of amulets, jewels, stones and talismans: one part of storax, one of frankincense, one of benzoin, and one of myrrh.

Incense for business success: two parts of benzoin, one of cinnamon, and one of basil.

Incense to cleanse the home of negative vibrations: three parts of frankincense, three of copal, two of myrrh, and one of sandalwood.

Incense to counteract curses and evil spells: two parts of sandalwood and one of bay leaf. This incense is burned for seven nights during the waning moon.

Incense to attract prophetic dreams: two parts of sandalwood, one of white rose petals, one of camphor, one of white lily, and a few drops of jasmine oil.

Incense to solve problems, dispel danger, and keep away disagreeable persons: three parts of frankincense, two of dragon's blood, two of myrrh, one of asafetida, one of pepper, one of rue, and one of garlic skin.

Incense of the moon: three parts frankincense, a part of sandalwood, and one of camphor.

Incense for business matters: two parts of benzoin, two of frankincense, one of lavender, and one of dried marjoram.

Incense to invoke spirits: one part of aniseed, one of coriander seed, and one of cardamom seed.

Incense to perceive visions: three parts of frankincense, one of bay leaf, and one of damiana. This incense is burned during meditations.

Universal incense: three parts of frankincense, two of benzoin, one of myrrh, one of sandalwood, and one of rosemary. This incense is used for all types of positive magic rituals, and to invoke cosmic forces.

Oils, Baths, and Sachet Bags

The most powerful and popular of the oils are known as essential oils because they are highly concentrated. One needs only a drop of an essential oil to perfume an entire room. The essential oils are especially used in aromatherapy lamps.

Witches prefer to prepare their own oils and infusions by boiling the appropriate herbs, flowers, or leaves of the fragrance they need. For example, rose oil is prepared by boiling rose petals in pure oils, such as jojoba, which may be found in stores that sell natural products. In the same manner, one may prepare cinnamon, lavender, gardenia, and mint oil, and many other fragrances. The advantage of making oils this way is that they are pure and do not contain any preservatives that may contaminate them. Perfumes may also be made by placing flowers or herbs in alcohol for several weeks. The alcohol with the flowers or herbs is kept in a tightly capped dark bottle. Afterwards the liquid is strained and the result is a pure and natural fragrance. The type of alcohol used is ethyl alcohol, not the isopropyl alcohol that is found in drugstores.

The herbs that are used must be dry because fresh herbs contain too much water and their aroma is diluted in the alcohol.

One of the most magical herbs is Dittany of Crete. It is not easy to find but some of the stores that specialize in exotic herbs sometimes carry it. Witches prepare a very powerful oil with Dittany of Crete that they use during astral travels. The oil is prepared by boiling equal parts of Dittany of Crete, cinnamon, jasmine, sandalwood, and benzoin in jojoba oil. This is a type of flying ointment that is said to transport a person to "other realms of existence." To use it it is necessary to rub the oil over the entire body. It is not dangerous or hallucinogenic, but it establishes a connection with the unconscious mind and helps the person enter into the trance that is a precursor to astral travel.

Another oil is very popular with some Witches is prepared by boiling sandalwood, cinnamon, carnation petals, and vervain in jojoba oil. The oil is kept in a receptacle marked on the outside with a pentagram. It is used to achieve total union with the Great Goddess or Cosmic Mother and her Divine Consort.

Witches prepare a special ointment to attract riches that is made with beeswax mixed with a few drops of patchouli oil, clove oil, basil oil, and oak oil. The oils are prepared beforehand by boiling the various herbs or spices in jojoba oil. This oil is rubbed on the hands every day. A sun ointment is similarly prepared for abundance, prosperity, and good health. This ointment is made by mixing beeswax with frankincense oil, orange oil and cinnamon oil. For love purposes beeswax is mixed with ylang-ylang oil, lavender oil, cardamom oil and vanilla extract. The ointment is rubbed over the entire body before a love encounter. For healing purposes, the beeswax is mixed with cedar oil, sandalwood oil, eucalyptus oil, and cinnamon oil. The ointment is rubbed over the entire body, but it should never be used on burns or open wounds. In the preparation of these ointments the beeswax is melted before it is mixed with the natural oils. After the mixture cools, the beeswax hardens again.

The moon ointment is also prepared with beeswax mixed with sandalwood oil, lemon oil, and rose oil. This ointment is said to help establish contact with the moon Goddess or Cosmic Mother and it is especially efficacious during Full moon rituals.

The Witch's flying ointment is very famous. During the Middle Ages people believed that Witches flew around on brooms, but in reality what they did was use the flying ointment. Because this ointment was made of hallucinogenic substances the Witches believed that they were flying. The next list provides two different formulas for the flying ointment. The first formula is extremely toxic and should never be used, as it is composed of several very dangerous drugs. The second formula is not toxic and may be used without any danger. It is not as potent as the first but it is said to be very effective.

Flying Ointment #1 (Toxic)

Aconite
Belladonna
Hemlock
Marijuana

Hashish
Parsley

The ingredients are crushed into powder and mixed with lard.

Flying Ointment #2 (Nontoxic)

Sandalwood oil
Jasmine oil
Benzoin
Ginger oil
Dittany of Crete

Dittany of Crete was mixed with the oils. Both formulas were rubbed over the entire body to obtain the sensation that the user was flying. During these imaginary flights the person had many hallucinations and extraordinary visions.

Both oils and ointments are used commonly in Wicca. Many Witches, who do not have the time to prepare their own oils, use essential oils. These oils are expensive as they are based on strong concentrations of each substance, but they are ideal in the practice of magic because they are not imitations. They may be found in most New Age stores. It is important to remember that Witches do all their magic through rituals and are very careful to observe the moon phases during their magic spells. Something that is as apparently straightforward as the preparation of oils is done in a ritualistic form in Wicca. Following is the ritualistic preparation of an oil believed to attract money to a person or a house.

Money Oil Formula

7 drops of patchouli oil
5 drops of cedar oil
4 drops of vetivert oil
2 drops of ginger oil
jojoba oil

The oil is made during the waxing moon. The Witch has already prepared a receptacle of sterilized glass. He stands in the east and begins to concentrate on money, large amounts of money that will come to him through the use of the oil. He then pours ⅛ of a cup of jojoba oil into the receptacle. As he continues to visualize the amount of money that he needs, he adds the seven drops of patchouli oil to the jojoba. (A dropper is always used to measure the oil.) He mixes the oils with a spoon that may be made of wood or plastic but not of metal. He smells the liquid and continues to visualize his need. Next he adds the cedar oil, stirs it, smells it, and keeps on visualizing. The money oil keeps getting stronger as he adds the ingredients and visualizes what he wants. Next comes the vetivert oil, which is also stirred and smelled. Lastly he adds the ginger oil. This oil is so powerful that only two drops need to be used. The Witch stirs and smells. The money oil is now ready. The Witch lifts the receptacle between his hands and presents it to the east, south, west and north, stating on each cardinal point that large amounts of money are coming to him through the use of the oil.

Next he waits for the night of the full moon, keeping the oil in a dark place. When the full moon arrives, he undresses completely, rubs some of the oil over his entire body, and visualizes that the money desired is swiftly flowing to him.

After the initial use of the oil, the Witch rubs it only on his palms every day. It is important to remember that when one tries to acquire money through magic the source of the money must never be stated. It is necessary to let the money come to the person in a natural form and from any source.

The money oil and all similar oils may also be used to anoint candles, crystals and stones, amulets, talismans, and sachet bags. The oils are also used in the bath, by placing only a few drops in the water to energize the aura.

Before we discuss the ritual baths used in Wicca, we should mention several methods to prepare the magic ink. As we saw earlier, the most popular formula for the ink uses benzoin, gum arabic, and dragon's blood mixed with ethyl alcohol. This ink is red and very powerful. Another formula calls for mixing gum arabic with beet juice. A very powerful formula for the ink uses the soot that may be found inside chimney walls or on the insides of empty candle glasses. This soot, which is very black, is mixed with a few drops of distilled water and gum arabic. This ink is very difficult to make as it stains everything it touches, but it is said to be extremely potent. Another type of magic ink is invisible ink, which is prepared by mixing lemon juice with a little milk.

All the magic inks are used with old-fashioned pens, of the type that is dipped in an inkwell, or preferably with a feather. The pen that is used must be purified beforehand by passing it through the four elements, symbolized by a red candle, water, incense, and salt.

The invisible ink is used in visualizations. When a Witch desires something he or she writes the wish on a piece of parchment paper with the invisible ink. Parchment paper is made of lambskin.

When the ink on the paper is dry, the message cannot be seen. The Witch looks at the blank paper for a few minutes and expresses his desire several times in a loud voice. He then lights a white candle and places the paper over it, being careful not to burn it. The heat of the flame will make the message reappear on the paper. When he sees the writing on the paper, the Witch states that in the same manner that the words have appeared on the paper, so will his wishes be materialized. This is a simple spell but it is said to be very effective.

The ritual baths used in Wicca are not boiled. They are prepared in pieces of fine linen. The cloth must be as transparent as possible and it must be white or colorless. In the middle of the cloth the Witch places a combination of herbs, depending on what he wishes to accomplish through the bath. It may be for dispelling negative vibrations, for love, good health, money, or good luck. As he mixes the herbs—which should be dried—he visualizes what he desires and expresses it aloud. He ties the cloth with a piece of cord and drops it into the bath water, which should be very hot. The herbs begin to emanate their energy as soon as they come in contact with the hot water. The Witch waits until the water has cooled and has become perfumed with the herbs. He then immerses himself into the bath, relaxes, and begins to visualize his desire. Some Witches use floating candles on the water to multiply its energies. When he has remained in the bath for at least half an hour, he ends the visualization and lets the water be drained, imagining that in the same manner all his problems are disappearing from his life. The herbs used in the baths are thrown away, and the cloth is rinsed and put away to use on another occasion. These baths are repeated during three, seven, or nine days depending on the Witch's need. As may be readily seen, this type of bath is more effective than the ones that are poured over the body because the influence of the herbs are in contact with the person for a longer period of time.

Following is a list of bath formulas for different needs.

Against Evil Spells

4 parts rosemary

3 parts spurge

2 parts bay leaf

1 part rue

For Love (aphrodisiacal)

3 parts red rose petals

2 parts rosemary

2 parts thyme

1 part myrtle

1 part jasmine or lily blossoms

1 part lavender

Against Addictions

2 parts rosemary

1 part lavender

1 part lemon leaves

1 part vervain

1 part sage

For Exorcisms

2 parts basil

2 parts rosemary

2 parts cumin

1 part rue

1 part spurge

For Love

3 parts red rose petals

2 parts cinnamon

2 parts vervain

2 parts myrtle

2 parts lavender

2 parts orange blossoms

For Money

3 parts patchouli

2 parts basil

1 part cinnamon

1 part cedar

For Purification Rituals

4 parts lavender

4 parts rosemary

3 parts thyme

3 parts basil

2 parts hyssop

1 part mint

1 part vervain

a pinch of valerian

To Develop Psychic Powers

3 parts lemon leaves

2 parts thyme

2 parts orange rinds

1 part cloves

1 part cinnamon

A Witch's Bath

3 parts rosemary

3 parts red carnation petals

2 parts galangal

2 parts cinnamon

1 part ginger

Witches also use fresh herbs for special cleansings. The herbs chosen are tied with a red ribbon and sprinkled with salt water. They are used to dispel negative influences in the home and in the room where rituals take place. The most common combination of herbs used in this type of cleansing is mint, marjoram, and rosemary.

Also very common in Wicca are small bags that are stuffed with herbs for different purposes. These are then inserted inside the Witch's pillow. For a restful sleep, the bags are filled with rosemary or spearmint. To drive away night-mares, aniseed is used. For prophetic dreams the bag is filled with bay leaf and a jade stone. For astral travels, as the person sleeps, the herbs used are vetivert, sandalwood, white rose petals, a vanilla bean, and a pinch of orris root. These bags are about three to four inches long and three inches wide.

Fruits are also used in Wicca for different purposes. A very powerful love spell is a pomander made of an orange completely studded with cloves. This pomander is used to attract the love of a man. To attract a woman's love a lemon is prepared in the same manner. The fruit is then placed in a bowl filled with a mixture of powdered cinnamon, brown sugar, powdered coriander, powdered ginger, powdered orris root, civet, and ambergris. The fruit is rolled in the mixture until it is well covered by it and left in the bowl for two weeks, rolling it inside the mixture every day. At the end of the two weeks the pomander is removed from the bowl and surrounded with seven pink candles anointed with cinnamon oil. The candles are lit for seven minutes, while the Witch visualizes that he or she is already enjoying the love of the person desired.

The Witch then ties a long pink ribbon to a large iron nail and drives the nail into the top of the pomander. The ribbon with the pomander is hung from the ceiling in a visible place. Every day the pomander is struck lightly with the hand, making it swing from the ribbon so that its powerful fragrance will permeate the room. This is a love spell of great power.

Sachet bags are also filled with powders, herbs, stones, amulets, talismans, and other ingredients. They are carried in a pocket or a handbag for protection and for help with many problems. They are also known as ouanga or jou-jou bags. Most of these bags are red as this color is a symbol of power and passion, but some Witches also use green or yellow sachet bags to attract money. Also common are black bags with Runes inside for the accumulation of power. Following is a list of sachet bags for different purposes.

For Love

Red sachet bag
Red rose petals
Vervain
Cinnamon
Adam and Eve root
Orris root
A rodochrosite
A fire opal
A rose quartz
Two magnets

The stones used in the sachet bags are unpolished to ensure greater potency. This also makes them more economical than the polished ones, which can be very expensive.

For Money

Green sachet bag
Patchouli
Cinnamon
Cumin

Cloves
Amber
Jade
Aventurine
Pyrite

To Win at Games of Chance

Green sachet bag
Patchouli
Nutmeg
Bay leaf
Lily blossom
A magnet
A green dice
A malachite
A piece of copper

To Protect a Car

Blue sachet bag
Rosemary
Basil
Vervain
A white quartz
A pinch of salt

For Protection When Traveling

Yellow sachet bag
Powdered mustard
Seaweed

Dragon's blood
Alum
A turquoise
An amethyst

To Acquire Riches

Cinnamon
Lemon leaves
A vanilla bean
A tonka bean
Cloves
A carborundrum
A pyrite
Clover leaves (or an amulet shaped like a four-leaf clover)

THE LEVANAH NECTAR

Magical potions and philters are also very popular in Wicca. One of these potions is known as the Levanah Nectar. Levanah is one of the magical names of the moon. The Levanah Nectar is made on both the new and the full moon to contact lunar forces and to acquire power and energy. The Nectar is prepared in the following manner.

The Nectar requires an egg white, half a cup of white wine, a dollop of half and half cream, and sugar to taste. The egg white is whipped until it is fluffy and the other ingredients are then added. The mixture is poured into a blue chalice with a silver pentagram drawn on its surface. There is a special blue chalice that is used for this purpose which has a pewter stem shaped like a half moon. It may be found in some New Age stores.

After the Nectar has been poured into the chalice, a moonstone is added to the mixture, which is placed where the moon may shine upon it. A silver candle is lit in front of the chalice, which is dedicated to the lunar forces and especially to the Great Goddess. The candle is allowed to burn for one hour and the Nectar is drunk, preferably facing the moon. This is repeated every new and full moon.

Witches are very careful in the preparation of their potions and they only use distilled or spring water to ensure their purity. Following is a list of some of the most popular potions and philters used in Wicca.

Aphrodisiacal Potion to Awaken Passion

Rosemary
Thyme
Tea leaves
Coriander seeds
Mint
5 pink rosebuds
5 lemon leaves
Nutmeg
Orange rind
Ginger

Three or four cups of water are boiled in a pan and the ingredients are added and allowed to steep for half an hour. Honey is added to sweeten the mixture, which should be drunk as hot as possible. It is said to be extremely aphrodisiacal.

Potion to Gain the Power of Clairvoyance

(It is not drunk; only the fumes are inhaled.)

Petals of white roses
Cinnamon

Nutmeg
Bay leaf
Dittany of Crete

Potion to Have Prophetic Dreams

Rose petals
Spearmint
Cinnamon
Jasmine blossoms

The ingredients are added to a cup of boiled water and allowed to steep for a half hour. The liquid is drunk before going to sleep.

Moon Water

A silver vessel is filled with distilled or spring water and placed where it may receive the rays of the full moon. This is done when the moon rises. The vessel is left in its place so that it may be illuminated by the moon the whole night. Just before sunrise the water is poured into a clay receptacle and closed tightly. It is kept where it may never get the light of the sun. This lunar water is marvelous to attract love, money, and to develop psychic powers. The hands and the brow are anointed with the liquid whenever the need arises.

Sun Water

A crystal vessel is filled with distilled or spring water, and placed where it may receive the sun's rays from sunrise to sunset. The water is poured into a sterilized bottle and capped tightly. This water is excellent for purification, energy, good health, and especially to attract money. It is used to sprinkle around the house three consecutive days every month. The bottle with the liquid is placed where it may receive the sun rays every day. It does not matter if it is also illuminated by moonlight.

Purification Formula

Nine magic herbs and flowers are mixed in a bowl, which must not be made of metal. Among the most popular are rosemary, vervain, rue, oak leaves, pine leaves, cassia, carnations, thyme, basil, jasmine, and spearmint.

Rain and spring waters are added to the plants, which are placed in a dark place, well covered, for three days. The liquid is then strained and poured into a tightly capped bottle. This water is excellent to sprinkle around the house and to rub over the entire body, as it is said to dispel impure vibrations and to drive away bad luck.

Formula to Protect a House

Rue
Rosemary
Vetivert
Hyssop
Mistletoe

The herbs are boiled in spring water and the strained liquid is used to anoint all the doors and windows of the house. The rest of the liquid is poured down the sink so that it may purify everything that exits the house. This liquid must not be taken internally.

Love Philter

A bottle of red wine
Cinnamon
Ginger
Vanilla

The ingredients are added to the bottle of wine. Three days later the wine is served to the person desired.

Formula Against Insomnia and Nightmares

White rose petals
Myrtle
Vervain

The rose petals are added to a vessel of spring water and left in the liquid for three days. Every day more petals are added to the water. The third day the myrtle and vervain are added to the liquid at sunrise. That evening the liquid is strained and poured into a tightly capped bottle. The liquid is rubbed three times on the forehead every night before going to sleep. This ensures a restful sleep, free of nightmares.

Formula for Witch's Honey

Two cups of honey
Cinnamon sticks
Cloves
A piece of sugared ginger
Lemon rind
Vanilla
A pinch of powdered cardamom

The ingredients are mixed and energized, charging them with thoughts of love, harmony, and the Witch's power. The honey is then poured into a crystal vessel and well covered. A pink candle is lit on each side of the vessel. When the candles are finished the honey is put away for three weeks before it is used.

War Water

This formula is used by Witches when they face a dangerous enemy against whom they wish to protect themselves. Three pounds of large iron nails are placed in a large pot of water, to which is added some rain water. The liquid is boiled for half an hour over a high flame. Then it is strained and poured into a dark bottle that is tightly capped. It is placed in a dark place for seven days. After this time, the hands, the feet, and the chest are rubbed with the liquid every day while the conflict lasts. This gives the Witch great power over his enemy and helps him win the struggle. War water is especially effective in court cases.

Candles and Their Uses

Candles are of primordial importance in all the rites of Wicca, as in all magical practices. Many Witches prefer to make their own candles because they believe that mass-market candles are not as effective. To make their own candles they begin by melting virgin wax and adding different vegetable dyes. Then they pour the hot wax on paraffin paper, add a long wick in the middle, and roll the wax in the paper to form a tube. They remove the candle from the paper and place it on a table to harden. They repeat this process several times until they have a large supply of candles. Then they cut the ends of the wick to a suitable length. They use the same method to make the color candles they use most often. What makes this long process so desirable is that they can add various magical ingredients, like herbs and spices, to the candles. In this manner they can make especial candles for love, money, and other magical purposes. Some Witches

only make white ritual candles in this way and use commer-
cial candles in their regular spells.

The following is list of color candles and their uses in
Wicca:

Red: for heath purposes, to increase energy, for sexual passion, and for courage, protection, and aid
against enemies.

Pink: for love, marriage, friendship, and relaxation.

Orange: for attraction, energy, and to gather beneficial influences.

Yellow: for developing the mind, for a divination,
communication, eloquence, and travels. It is also
believed to help in schoolwork.

Green: for money, prosperity, employment, promotions, fertility, and growth.

Light Blue: for healing, peace, patience, psychic abilities, and joy. It is also believed to be an aid
against insomnia.

Indigo: for abundance, prosperity, bank loans, and
to acquire the help of powerful persons.

Violet: for power, to contact higher entities and to
heal serious illnesses. Seven violet candles lit in a
circle around a person's photograph are said to
give control over that individual if he or she does
not know how to counteract the spell.

White: for protection, spirituality, and all magical
purposes.

Black: to dispel negative influences or to absorb
them. Black candles are also used in spells of

death and destruction. Some Witches recommend lighting black candles when a person is mortally ill to absorb destructive vibrations.

Brown: to destroy evil spells and to heal domestic animals.

Many Witches do not use matches to light their candles because matches are made of sulphur, which is believed to have negative vibrations. Others prefer the use of matches because they believe lighters decrease the power of fire.

Saltpeter is a very popular substance in Wicca. A pinch of saltpeter sprinkled over the flame of a candle will make it jump and give up sparks. It is believed that this enhances the energy of the flame.

During many rituals and spells candles are only allowed to burn for a certain period of time, usually an hour. The next day the candle is relit for the same purpose. This repetitive process is said to be more effective than letting the candle burn itself out the first time it is lit. An exception to this rule are glass-encased candles, which are usually allowed to burn themselves out completely. There are also in the market candles made of seven or nine "knots." The knots are small balls of wax which are stacked upon each other. They can be found in various colors, especially red for love and green for money. A "knot" is lit each day until the candle is finished. A petition is made each time one of the knots is lit.

Candles are never blown out in Wicca. They are extinguished with the fingers or with a candle snuffer. This is done because blowing the candle sets the Air element against the Fire element. Christian churches also use candle snuffers.

Candles are anointed with special oils before lighting them. It is important to remember that candles have a north pole (the base) and a south pole (the tip). For this reason the candles must not be rubbed up and down during its anointing so that its polarity will not be destroyed. Instead, they are anointed, from the middle downwards and from the middle upwards. This energizes and increases the candle's polarity. Candles are placed in candleholders, although small dishes are sometimes used.

Following are various simple candle rituals used in Wicca.

To Heal an Illness

Three light blue and three violet candles are lit in a circle around the photograph of the person who is ill. Before the candles are lit each is held in the hands, charging it with healing thoughts for the person. Then they are all lit and allowed to burn themselves out completely. The ritual is repeated during three days at the same time.

To Bind a Candle

This ritual is conducted to bind money or to attract it, or to acquire something that is desired. The candle is placed in a candleholder, using green for money, pink for love, indigo for prosperity, or violet to heal an illness. Before lighting the candle it is held between the hands and energized mentally, expressing aloud what the person wishes to bind. One of the oil formulas previously given may be used to anoint the candle, according to what is desired. A cord or ribbon of the same color as the candle is held between the hands and stretched tightly so that it is tense. While holding the cord or ribbon in this manner, the person repeats what he or she wishes to accomplish. Then the candle is tied in the middle and a knot is made while chanting: The spell is cast, the candle bound; evil has passed, and joy is found. A second knot is made and the words of the spells are chanted again. This is repeated seven times. The candle is lit and allowed to burn until it reaches the cord or ribbon, at which point it is extinguished. This is done during twenty-one days with a new candle and cord.

For Love

The initials of the person desired are drawn on a piece of pink cloth. The initials of the one who wishes his or her love are drawn over them. A heart made of red cloth is sewn over the initials and covered with cinnamon, brown sugar, and pink rose petals. A pink candle on its candleholder is lit over the heart. Love oil may be used to anoint the candle beforehand. The candle is lit one hour daily until it is finished. Each time the candle is lit these words are chanted: "Love for me burns in your heart, we will never be apart." After the candle is finished, all the ingredients and what is left of the candle are wrapped in the pink cloth and buried near the home of the person desired or where he or she goes by often.

Birthday Candle

At sunrise on his birthday, the person inscribes his name on a silver candle with a new nail. Then he anoints it with a mixture of mineral oil, powdered camphor, powdered alum, white sugar, and silver dust. He writes his most cherished wish on a piece of silver paper. He then lights the candle five minutes every hour of that day, while reading the wish. A few minutes before midnight he goes to a window where he can see the sky and preferably the moon. He lifts the unlit candle between the hands and says, "White Goddess, Beloved Mother, grant me my wish on this solemn day and give me your blessing." He lights the candle again, burns the paper in its flame, and lets the candle be finished.

For Money

A long green candle is anointed with a mixture of mineral oil, bay leaf, mint, cinnamon, and cumin. It is placed in a candleholder and surrounded with seven silver coins. It is lit for one hour and extinguished over one of the coins. The next day it is lit again for an hour and extinguished over another of the coins. This is repeated during seven days, extinguishing the candle over a different coin each time. The last day the candle is relit after being extinguished, is allowed to burn itself out. The coins are kept inside a green sachet bag, which is placed under the mattress to multiply money.

To Overcome an Enemy

A red candle is anointed with a mixture of mineral oil, dragon's blood, paprika, and a pinch of asafetida. The candle is tied from top to bottom with red thread, until it is completely covered. The candle is lit while saying the following words:

> *You want war and I want peace*
> *Through the power of this candle*
> *all your evil will now cease.*

The candle is allowed to burn itself out and the ritual is repeated over three days at the same time with a new candle. Then a white candle is anointed with mineral oil, sugar, and powdered camphor and carried throughout the entire house, visualizing that the enemy is controlled by positive forces and cannot do any further evil.

For World Peace

A white candle is anointed with a mixture of mineral oil, powdered alum, hyssop, rose oil, gardenia oil, and sugar. It is surrounded with four white quartz crystals in the form of a cross. The crystals must have fine points and be as clear as possible.

The planet Earth is visualized surrounded by a great white light that is emitted by the four crystals. The candle is lit and the Great Goddess is petitioned to envelop the planet with her mantle of love and peace. The candle is allowed to burn itself out and the ritual is repeated during seven days with a new candle. This ritual is especially effective when there is war or the threat of war anywhere on the planet.

THE MAGIC MIRROR

Witches use many forms of divination, such as the Runes, the tarot cards, the crystal ball, and especially the Magic Mirror, also known as the Black Mirror. This method of divination is known as "scrying." There are scrying mirrors in the market, but most Witches prefer to make their own. To prepare the mirror, the Witch finds a large round piece of glass, preferably concave. He covers the outer side with black matte paint. The concave part will reflect the black color but with the slight sheen of its glass surface. This is the Black Mirror. Before using it, it must be consecrated with the four elements: Earth, Water, Fire, and Air. The Witch places some salt into the concave part of the mirror and says: "By the power of the Great Goddess and her Consort, the Great God, I consecrate you in the Earth element." He empties the salt and fills the mirror with spring water and says: "By the power of the Great Goddess and her Consort, the Great God, I consecrate you in the Water element." He continues the consecration, passing the mirror over the flame of a red candle representing the Fire element, and incense smoke representing the Air element. During each consecration, he repeats the same words but uses the name of the other elements.

After the Black Mirror has been consecrated in the four elements, it is exposed to the rays of the waxing moon, starting the night of the New Moon and ending on the full moon. Once the Black Mirror is ready, the Witch has a powerful divination tool of great magical qualities at his disposal.

To use the Black Mirror, the Witch fills it with water or oil. He places it on his altar between two white candles. He lights the candles and turns off all the lights in the room. He then proceeds to "scry" or visualize on the surface of the mirror. He concentrates on each question or thing he desires to know and observes intently the images that form on the mirror's surface or the mental messages he receives from his unconscious through the power of the mirror. As we saw earlier, it is possible to buy a ready-made scrying mirror but it must also be consecrated in the four elements and exposed to the moon's rays. The element consecration must always be done during the waxing moon.

THE CRYSTAL BALL

Some Witches alternate the use of the Magic Mirror with the Crystal Ball. There are several types of divination balls and the most common are made of ordinary glass. These are always completely clear and transparent but they do not have the same power as the true crystal ball, which is made of white quartz.

In the following list of stones we will discuss in some detail the powers of the white quartz. This is a very powerful stone because of its ability to register and record every impression it receives. It is also said to have powerful connections with the higher realms. A large quartz ball that is completely transparent would be tremendously expensive. The cheaper ones contain crystal inclusions in their interior, having only some areas that are transparent. The inclusions found in white quartz are identified as spiritual entities that inhabit the heart of the stone. For that reason many Witches prefer crystal balls with inclusions over the transparent ones because they consider them to be more valuable magically.

The price of a crystal ball depends on its size. The larger they are, the higher their cost. Once a Witch has acquired the ball he wants, he submerges it for twenty-four hours in a solution of spring water and sea salt. Then he rinses it and exposes it to sunlight for at least six hours to re-energize it. After it has been purified and energized, he consecrates it in the four elements in the same manner as the Magic Mirror, and exposes it to the rays of the waxing moon.

The Crystal Ball is used like the Magic Mirror, placing it between two lit white candles in a darkened room. It must be placed on a holder over a black cloth to avoid unwanted reflections. The hands are placed on each side of the Ball so that it may receive the Witch's personal vibrations. The same way the quartz records impressions it can also project them upon its surface, making them visible to whoever is looking at it.

In contrast with the Magic Mirror, the Witch seeks forms and images in the Crystal Ball which he then interprets psychically. Clouds may be formed in the crystal and its inclusions may take special shapes that have a definite meaning for the Witch. Some Witches use the Crystal Ball most commonly to read for their clients. The Magic Mirror is mostly used for personal matters and in more complicated situations. It is rarely used to read another person's fortune.

STONES, QUARTZ, AND THEIR USES

itches use different types of precious and semi-precious stones in their magic spells. Among these the most popular is the white quartz, but other stones, like amber, amethyst, moonstone, agate, and jet are also used. The ritualistic necklace worn by the High Priestess is made of amber and jet beads, alternating the beads until the necklace is completed.

Following is a list of the most common stones used in Wicca.

Agate: this is one of the most common and more used stones used in magic and in chakra therapy. The agate is a solar stone of great energy. One of its most common uses is in the form of a disk which is placed on the solar plexus to improve the health and to attract money. Agates come in various colors, such as cream, blue, red, and green, but sometimes they are dyed. There are also several types of this stone, like moss agate, that seems to have herbs in its interior. Dendrite agate is excellent as a protection during travels. This stone is white with dark or blue "stars" in its depths. Lace agate exists in several colors. The blue-lace type is excellent to soothe the nerves if it is rubbed repeatedly between the hands.

Alexandrite: this is a crystalline stone of a greenish-violet shade which has blue or yellow rays in its midst. It is said to attract love, good luck, and to establish strong connections with superior forces. It is also used to develop psychic abilities.

Amazonite: this is a solid stone, not crystalline, of a light aquamarine color with white inclusions. It is excellent for communication, and attracts friendship and creativity. It helps heal throat ailments, thyroid problems, and nervous complaints.

Amber: this is a resin formed from the crystallized sap of trees during millions of years. It gives power, wisdom, and is excellent to attract love and money, especially when combined with jade or aventurine. Amber may be found in yellow, red, or light green hues. It may be clear or have inclusions of herbs or insects in its depths.

Amethyst: is a deep violet color and it is highly mystical. It helps develop telepathy, intuition, and clairvoyance. It is also used often in love spells. If it is placed in liquor and drunk, it helps cure alcohol addiction. It also helps cure other addictions, like drugs, overeating, and sexual excesses.

Angelite: when placed on the throat for a half hour before sleep, it is said to help contact the person's guardian angel. It is pale blue, solid, and has white spots on its surface that resemble cloud formations.

Apache tear: this is black stone of the obsidian family. It is used in love spells to make an unfaithful lover "cry" with remorse. It is also excellent to cure depression, especially when caused by the loss of loved ones.

Aqua aura: this is an aquamarine transparent stone that is excellent in meditations and to attract love and peace.

Aquamarine: it belongs to the beryllium family. It is aqua blue, translucent, and very popular in spells for love, peace, and prosperity. It also helps in heart ailments and strengthens the immunity system.

Aventurine: is dark green and belongs to the quartz family. It soothes violent emotions, dispels fear, and calms those who carry it on their persons. It is used especially to attract good luck in business deals.

Jet: is black, lusterless, and used to dispel the evil eye, evil spells, and to protect against negative vibrations. When combined with coral, it is very effective in the protection of infants, especially when it is carved in the form of a ficca, which is a closed fist with the thumb protruding between the index and middle fingers. Witches form the ficca with their right hand and use it to cast the magic circle when the athame or magic wand are not available.

Azurite: this is a many-pointed stone, of a vivid blue color and often has violet highlights. It helps develop the "third eye" which is located between the eyes, and also gives psychic powers. It helps heal sinusitis and nervous complaints.

Moonstone: this stone is an opalescent albite from the feldspar family. It is found on the moon in large quantities and that gives it its name. It is of a cream color with pink and gray highlights. It is used in spells associated with the moon, and is one of the ingredients in the Nectar of Levanah. It may be used to bring back persons or to establish contact with those who live far away.

Goldstone (also Sunstone): this is a bright semi-transparent stone of a honey color with many golden points in its interior. It is excellent for magic spells.

Bloodstone: is a deep green shade with red spots. It is associated with Aries and is very popular in the healing of blood diseases and circulatory problems. It is used in money spells. It is also electromagnetic and gives great energies to those who carry it on their persons.

Bodji Stones: they are made of iron and magnetite and are used in pairs. They must be exposed to sunlight often to multiply their energies. They are said to soothe arthritic pain if held in the hands for long periods of time. They also help balance the body's electromagnetic field.

Leopard Stone: so called because it is yellow with brown spots that resemble a leopard's skin. It is found very commonly in "egg" form and is used in love spells, especially for unfaithful lovers.

Calcite: the most common color of this stone is yellow but it may also be found in orange, green, white, and blue shades. It rids the body of toxins and vitalizes it. It also helps heal bone diseases and problems with the spinal cord.

Carborundrum: this is an exquisite rocky black stone with iridescent highlights and only exists in outer space in its natural form. It was created by coincidence in a laboratory by a scientist who was trying to produce diamonds from coal. For this reason the carborundrum is said to be a cousin of the diamond. Carborundrum is an abrasive and is the most powerful stone that may be used to attract riches, abundance, and prosperity.

Carnelian: is a bright red-orange color and belongs to the jasper family. It is excellent to stimulate passion, to attract love, and to improve sexual relationships. It also stimulates the appetite and helps improve digestion. Some people use it to help heal diseases of the reproductive system and to ease menstrual cramps.

Celestite: is a light blue color, rocky, and crystalline. It is one of the stones most commonly used to develop spirituality. It is said to bring peace, serenity, and to ease worries.

Chrysocolla: is a bright aqua blue color with green highlights. It is one of the most powerful stones used to attract love between two persons and to reunite distanced lovers because it promotes feelings of peace and forgiveness.

Citrine: it belongs to the quartz family. It is crystalline, of a dark yellow color. It is excellent in money spells. When large pieces of this stone are placed around the house or business, it ensures prosperity, riches, and abundance. It also strengthens will power and dispels anxiety and fear. It is also said to improve the memory.

Coral: its most common color is red, but it may be also found in pink, white, and black shades. It is a living entity when it is in the sea and is marvelous in love spells.

White quartz: this is the most popular of all the stones used in magical practices. It is crystalline and transparent with inclusions and is also known as rock crystal. White quartz is highly magnetic and of great piezoelectric resonance. For this reason it is used in computers, radios, watches, telescopes, satellites, and in every field of technology. Because it receives and records all types of vibrations it must be purified before using it in spells or meditations. To purify it, it is placed in a solution of water and sea salt during twenty-four hours and then rinsed and exposed to sunlight for a minimum of six hours. It is placed on the forehead or held between the hands during meditations and inside sachet bags to attract love, money, and good luck. It is also very popular in healings and visualizations. It may be programmed by placing it between the eyes and expressing aloud what is desired to accomplish through its use. White quartz may be found in single or multiple points and sometimes in tumbled form. It is formed in its matrix with six natural facets. There are many types of white quartz, such as the river quartz, the phantom quartz which has shadows in its midst, the rutilated quartz which has golden fibers running through it, and the smoke quartz which has grayish hues. Many other stones grow within the white quartz matrix such as pyrite, which is a powerful money stone, and green tourmaline, also excellent for money and prosperity. Crystal water, which is excellent to help heal many illnesses, is prepared by placing a purified, single-point white quartz in a glass of spring water. It is left in the water during twenty-four hours and the liquid is then drunk on an empty stomach. This is repeated daily and it has helped cure many ailments.

Rose Quartz: of a light pink hue, this quartz is very effective in all love magic. It may be found in New Age stores in the shape of polished hearts. A rose pink heart placed on the chest energizes the heart chakra and helps heal heart ailments.

Desert Rose: it is white with light brown markings and is formed in clusters that resemble rose bunches. It is said to promote peace between lovers and married couples.

Diamond: it is considered to be the most precious of all stones. It is crystalline, although there are yellow and blue diamonds. The Herkimer diamond is very popular in the practice of magic because it is very inexpensive. This stone brings money and prosperity to its owner. Diamond jewels must be received as presents. If they are bought for personal wear, they are said to bring back good luck to their owner. Diamonds give peace, self-assurance, and self-control.

Emerald: is crystalline, a deep green color. It is associated with Taurus and the planet Venus. Emeralds attract love, money, and joy to their owners, especially if they are unpolished. In magic it is used in combination with a piece of pure copper, the metal of Taurus and Venus.

Fluorite: is crystalline, a deep green color highlighted with pink and violet. It is excellent to attract love and is used on the heart chakra to alleviate heart problems.

Garnet: is dark red, and associated with Capricorn and Scorpio. It grants balance, power, and great cosmic energy; it also attracts love and passion between lovers.

Hematite: is black with silver highlights. It is a magnetic stone associated with Capricorn and is excellent for business deals, inheritances, money, and to destroy evil spells and negative influences. It also gives balance and energy to the body. When surrounded by magnets these will adhere to the hematite because of its powerful magnetic field. It is used in bracelets, necklaces, and anklets for protection against dangers and enemies.

Jade: this is one of the most mystical stones used in magic. Its most popular color is light green, but it may also be found in pink, white, and black. Jade in combination with amber is excellent to attract money and prosperity. It is believed to prolong life. When placed inside the pillow it gives prophetic dreams.

Jasper: is a form of quartz, and belongs to the family of the chalcedony. It is found in yellow, orange, green and brown, and is used to help heal ailments connected with the gall bladder, the stomach, and the intestines. It gives great balance and is said to prolong life.

Kunzite: is light pink and very cherished by persons who heal with their hands. It gives unconditional love, strengthens the nervous system, and brings peace and spirituality to those who carry it.

Labradorite: is an iridescent light green. The darker shades are known as spectrolites. It is especially effective to find employment and secure promotions.

Lapedolite: this is a form of mica of a pink shade highlighted with light gray. It helps heal many illnesses, including cancer, if it is rubbed over the affected area daily.

Lapis lazuli: this is a beautiful bright blue stone with golden filaments of pyrite surrounding it. It was the favorite stone among the Egyptian pharaohs because of its alleged mystical powers. Lapis lazuli is associated with Sagittarius and is used between the eyes to help develop the third eye. In magic it is used to attract money. When this stone is used in combination with carborundrum it is said to bring riches and abundance to a house. The two stones are best placed in an abalone shell for added power.

Malachite: of a deep, bright green, this stone has concentric circles on its surface. It is wonderful to attract money and good luck. It may be used over the heart chakra to energize it and is said to protect infants against dangers when placed under the mattress of their cribs.

Moldavite: this is a type of meteorite of a light green color. It is an extremely powerful stone and is used over the forehead to contact cosmic forces.

Meteorite: there are various types of meteorite, like moldavites and tektites, which are light, of a dull black color. Tectites are created when the ground is melted by the impact of larger meteorites. The metal meteorites are made of solid iron and are extremely heavy. All meteorites are used in transcendental magic to contact powerful cosmic forces and to develop the third eye and acquire psychic abilities.

Obsidian: this is one of the stones associated with Capricorn and is excellent to attract money, for protection, to strengthen will power, and to balance the body. It protects against evil spells, negative vibrations, and drives away sorrow. It is black with iridescent green hues in its interior.

Onyx: is black and extremely brilliant. It is excellent to neutralize evil and grants great magical powers to its owner. It protects against sorceries, curses, and dark entities.

Opal: this is a precious stone of a milky white hue with fiery highlights in its center. It is associated with Libra. Only those born under this sign can wear opal jewels. Other signs attract tears and unhappiness to themselves when they wear this powerful stone. Opals are excellent for love spells because Libra, like Taurus, is ruled by Venus. The fire opal, especially, is marvelous for reuniting lovers.

Peridot: is crystalline, a light green shade, and is associated with Leo. It gives great protection to its owner and attracts money and abundance.

Pyrite: this metallic stone is rocky and resembles gold. During the gold rush it was known as fool's gold. It is the main stone used in money spells and for prosperity. It is used in many types of magic, including sachet bags.

Rhodocrosite: is bright pink with circles and intricate designs in a deeper shade of pink. This beautiful stone is excellent in all types of love spells because it promotes fidelity between lovers and gives permanency to love relationships.

Ruby: a deep, rosy red, this crystalline stone is associated with Aries and Leo. It is used in many love spells and gives great psychic powers to its owner. It attracts good luck in games of chance, as well as prosperity and abundance. In its unpolished form it is one of the most powerful ingredients of love sachet bags.

Selenite: is associated with the Moon and Cancer. It is a beautiful, semitransparent, mirror-like stone that is wonderful to contact lunar forces. Selenite mirrors are large pieces of this stone that are used to peer at the full moon through their depths. This is a very effective form of divination and very popular with some Witches. When it is carried in a love sachet bag it ensures the fidelity of a lover or spouse.

Sodalite: is a deep blue with white markings and is associated with Sagittarius. It helps develop psychic powers when placed daily on the third eye. It also attracts prosperity and abundance, especially when combined with lapis lazuli.

Sugilite: this rare stone is deep violet and may be found with black, pink, or white markings. It is known as the master stone as it connects other stones and magnifies their power. It is difficult to find as it is comes from a very small mine in

Africa. When placed on the throat chakra, it is said to establish a powerful connection with the guardian angel.

Tiger-eye: it is associated with Leo and is orange with iridescent streaks of the same color. It is carried in sachet bags to attract money.

Topaz: a semiprecious stone, it is bright yellow and crystalline and associated with Scorpio and Leo. It is excellent to attract money, prosperity, and love. It brings success in all endeavors, especially when used in its unpolished form.

Tourmaline: this is one of the most powerful and magical stones used in magic. It enhances the power of all magic spells and is especially cherished for its ability to contact superior forces. The most common of the tourmalines is black and is used to dispel sorrow and depression. The stone also comes in green and the popular melon and pink hues. The melon tourmaline is the most valuable of the family and also the most expensive, as well as the most powerful. It develops and strengthens all the chakras. When carried in a green sachet bag, it ensures a steady flow of money to its owner.

Turquoise: a bright aqua blue, this is Sagittarius' traditional stone. It attracts money, prosperity and abundance and protects against all dangers. It also helps develop psychic powers. It is the preferred stone of Native Americans because of its great mystical powers. Turquoise jewels are excellent for good luck and success in all endeavors. It must always be set in silver.

Sapphire: of a deep crystalline blue, this precious jewel is the most spiritual of all stones. It is associated with Virgo. It is said that God's throne is topped by a gigantic sapphire, which adds to the myths surrounding this powerful stone. Sapphires, polished or unpolished, bring good luck, money, and love to their owners, as well as protection against all evil.

Stones are used alone or in combination inside sachet bags and in all types of magic. Herbs and other magical substances are added to the bags to multiply their power. By using this list of stones, and the list of herbs and other ingredients already given, the reader may prepare his or her own sachet bags and create special spells according to his or her needs or desires.

SPELLS AND RITUALS

Most of Wicca's rituals take place during the Sabbaths, the annual festivals and the Esbats. The lunar phases are carefully observed during all rituals and ceremonies. The preferred day for the most important ceremonies is the full moon. The waning moon is used for cleansing rites, to dispel evil spells, or to overcome an enemy. The waxing moon is used for rituals and spells pertaining to positive magic, and to attract love, money, or anything important the Witch may desire. Witches will never carry out any type of positive magic during the waning moon.

The aspects between the planets and the signs which the sun occupies from month to month are also taken into consideration. The element that rules each ritual is also of great importance. Witches often work with elementals or entities that belong to a specific element, as we have already seen. One of the ways in which they contact elementals is the ritual dance, which is very effective in gathering great amounts of energy. This energy is then used during the rituals or spells. For example, to activate their cosmic energies, some Witches perform ritualistic dances with the help of drum rhythms or fast music. As they gyrate frenetically, they visualize their auras being replenished with vast amounts of energy. When they consider that they have accumulated sufficient energy through the dance, they proceed to use it by sending it mentally to accomplish their intended goal. They can also send this energy to a specific individual whom they desire to influence.

This is done by sending a mental command to that person together with the energy. This ritual may also be used to send healing energies to someone at a distance.

Once the Witch has ascertained that the moon phase, the zodiac sign, and the aspects between planets are auspicious for the magic he wants to do, he proceeds with the ritual or spell. Following is a list of several of the rituals and spells used in Wicca.

The Ritual of the Mirror and the Brush

This ritual is conducted by Witches to acquire power that later is directed to whatever they desire to accomplish. The Witch begins by donning a tunic of the adequate color. She turns off the lights in the room and lights a candle of the color that corresponds to the type of magic intended. For example, green for money, yellow for good health, red for passion, pink for love or marriage, and blue for success in all endeavors.

The Witch burns the adequate incense and sits down in front of the candle. Behind the candle she places a round mirror where she may see her face. As she looks at her image in the mirror, she proceeds to brush her hair repeatedly. As she brushes her hair, she says the following:

O Lady of transcendental beauty
For whom the stars are her most precious jewels,
And the universe her creation and delight;
You who weave human destinies
And protect all that is wild and free,
Hearken to me now,
Gather me within your being
And grant me your wonderful power.
Grant me this wish as I am your Witch and Priestess.
Grant me internal and external strength,
Eternal as the unbounded ocean.
Grant me the profound peace of my power
So that all may carry out my wishes;
And the wind, the water, and the fire
And the very mountains
Bow before me.
As I belong to the ancient wisdom,
Grant me the wisdom of all time
And the knowledge of light and darkness.
Grant me beauty ever perfect
And the power of seduction
So that I may mirror you with increasing splendor.
Create magic in me,
Create power in me.

The last two phrases, "Create magic in me, create power in me," are repeated by the Witch as she continues to brush her hair. This is done for a long period of time as the Witch feels the magic and the power of the Great Goddess grow steadily within her. When she thinks that she has accumulated the necessary energy, she concentrates all her mental power on what she wishes to accomplish. She then inhales deeply and exhales the air over the candle flame, extinguishing it. At that moment, whatever she has asked for is granted. As with all important rituals, the moon must be waxing and preferably full.

The Magic Link

Witches believe strongly in the power of objects that have been in contact with a person or which are associated with that person in some way.

This is known as contact magic or sympathetic magic. For example, used clothes, a used handkerchief, sweat, saliva, semen, nail clippings, hair, blood, and even the footsteps left by a person on the ground may be used to influence that person through magic means. This is known as the magic link. If none of these things is available, the name of the person, his birth date, his magical number, his zodiac sign, and the herbs, incenses, and colors associated with him may be used instead. These are of great help to cast an effective spell directed towards that person.

To Obtain a Man's Love

There are many types of spells that may be used for this purpose. For example, if the Witch is able to procure some of the desired man's hair, she will bind it to some of her own hair with a red ribbon. She then passes the mixed hair several times through one of the love incenses we have previously discussed. A popular love incense may be prepared by mixing powdered cinnamon, musk, powdered orris root, civet, and ambergris. The mixture is burnt over a lit charcoal. As the hair is passed through the incense the Witch commands that as her hair and that of her beloved are united, so will their persons be united in love and desire. The tied hair is placed in a red sachet bag together with a rose quartz and a magnet. The Witch carries the bag over her chest during seven days. At the end of this time, she must try to touch the one desired. As soon as the person has been touched, he will fall under the spell's influence. That evening, at the stroke of midnight, the hair must be burned in the flame of a red candle. The ashes are placed in contact with the desired person or sprinkled where he will step on them. The rose quartz and the magnet will continue to be carried inside the sachet bag.

To Ensure that a Husband or a Lover Does Not Stray

Another love spell used to restrain a philandering husband or lover employs the insoles of a pair of his shoes. The two insoles are rubbed with a bit of honey and cinnamon and nailed side by side on the floor of the woman's closet. A pair of her shoes are firmly placed over the insoles and never removed. This places the man under the woman's foot in a very effective manner.

To Obtain the Love of an Indifferent Man

When a husband or lover begins to show signs of a cooling passion, the woman cajoles him into a sexual interlude and gathers his semen carefully in a piece of cotton. She fills a small dish with olive oil, and adds a drop of blood from her middle finger, iron dust, dragon's blood, and a pinch of paprika. She works the cotton with the semen into a wick and places it over the oil. When the cotton is well soaked in the oil, she lights it an hour daily during seven days, adding more oil if needed. Many Witches believe this to be one of the most potent spells to reawaken passion in a man.

To Cool a Love Relationship

To bring about coldness between two lovers, their names are written on two pieces of unlined white paper and placed in the middle of a lime that has been cut in four equal parts but without letting them separate totally. The four lime slices with the paper inside are gathered together and kept in place by piercing them with forty-nines new pins. The lime is then placed inside a small jar together with ammonia, asafetida, valerian, and black pepper. The jar is capped tightly and placed in the freezer. This must be done during the waning moon for more effectiveness. It may be added that some Witches frown on this spell, which they feel borders on the darker side of magic.

To Get a Bank Loan

Not even the great banking institutions escape the power of the Witch. For example, if a Witch wishes to obtain a loan from a bank, he obtains an envelope or a paper with the name of the institution. Even a deposit slip may be used. He takes the paper home and places it over a piece of blue cloth, the color of triumph and prosperity. Over the paper he lights a blue candle anointed with olive oil which has been previously boiled with bay leaf, cinnamon, and chamomile flowers. He surrounds the paper with a circle of sugar and twenty-one coins that he obtained from the bank. He burns prosperity incense and passes it over the candle. He then places his hands on each side of the candle and proceeds to enchant it with the following words:

> *By the power of the fire*
> *and the Goddess of the Moon*
> *All the money I desire*
> *is coming to my hands soon.*
> *This bank will grant my petition*
> *through the Moon and through the Sun.*
> *Three knots fulfill my ambition,*
> *with three knots the spell is done.*

These words are chanted three times and immediately the Witch blows out the candle with one breath and makes three knots on the blue cloth with the bank's paper, the candle, the sugar, and the twenty-one coins inside. He passes the bundle through the incense again and puts it away in a safe place. This is a very powerful spell to obtain a bank loan and must be done during the waxing moon, preferably when it is full.

These are examples of spells done through a magic link but Witches do many powerful magic spells without it.

One of the most magical substances used by the Witches in their spells is the Condenser Fluid.

Condenser Fluid

The formula for this powerful liquid was first revealed by the famed German magician Franz Bardon. It was made popular by the well-known English Witch Sybil Leek, who strongly recommended it and who also gave the formula in one of her books.

To make the Condenser Fluid one begins by boiling a handful of chamomile flowers in a gallon of water. The pot where the infusion is boiled must be tightly covered so that none of the liquid escapes through evaporation. The water is allowed to boil during twenty minutes and then the liquid is strained using a piece of fine linen. The strained liquid is returned to the pot and boiled for another twenty minutes. It is then removed from the fire and after it has cooled, it is measured and alcohol in the same quantity is added to it. The next ingredients to be added to this liquid are ten drops of gold tincture and a drop of blood from the one preparing it. The liquid is poured into a dark bottle and placed where the sun's rays will not reach it.

The gold tincture is not difficult to prepare. It is made by diluting a gram of gold chloride in twenty grams of distilled water. The gold chloride may be found in chemical laboratories or in photographic laboratories, as this liquid is used in photographic paper.

After the Condenser Fluid has been prepared, it can be used in four different ways, according to the four elements. When it is used with the Air element, the magical influence takes place through evaporation. With the Fire element, the influence is through combustion. With the Water element, a liquid mixture is used. With the Earth element, the influence is through decomposition.

The Condenser Fluid works so rapidly that it is astonishing. Once, in Vienna, two Austrian friends of mine and I decided to use the Condenser Fluid through the Air element to bring someone to us. We began by filling a small cauldron with a little water and then added ten drops of the Condenser. As the Air element functions through evaporation, we placed the cauldron over a gas lamp, of the type used in camping trips. We joined our hands over the liquid and began to call the person mentally to us. Suddenly, in the middle of the water, we saw small lightning bolts crisscrossing from one side of the cauldron to the other. We looked at one another, stupefied, but continued to concentrate on the person. Suddenly somebody knocked at the door. I rose to open it and was astounded to see standing at the door the person we had been concentrating on.

I kept the person outside for a few minutes while my friends rushed around the room removing the cauldron and the gas stove and hiding them from view. Less than ten minutes had passed from the moment we started our invocation with the Condenser Fluid and the arrival of the person at the door. This is an extraordinary example of the effectiveness of the Condenser Fluid through the Air element. In this case, three persons conducted the magic ritual, but one person can also do the rite with the same results, provided he or she has strong powers of visualization.

To use the Condenser with the Fire element, one writes what is desired with a pencil on a piece of parchment paper.

The paper is soaked well in the Condenser and allowed to dry. Then it is burned with the flame of a red candle, visualizing that the desire has already come to pass.

It is important to remember that these are rituals of great power. For that reason, the room must be protected with a magic circle which may be made with the athame or the ficca. As we have already discussed, the ficca is made by making a fist and placing the thumb between the index and middle fingers. The incense corresponding to the element used should also be burned and the moon must be waxing.

To use the Condenser with the Water element, a small bowl is filled with distilled or spring water and ten drops of the Condenser are added to the liquid. The desired goal is strongly visualized for several minutes. The water is then poured into a clean bottle and brought immediately to a river or running stream where the bottle is emptied. This is the most popular use of the Condenser for magic spells.

To use the Condenser with the Earth element, an apple is cored and filled with ten drops of the Condenser. One then concentrates strongly on what is desired, and the apple is then buried in the ground. This method is used mostly when one wishes to contact a person who lives far away and also for money matters.

There are many simpler spells and rituals in Wicca, but none as powerful as the ones that use the Condenser Fluid.

To Separate a Lover from a Rival

This is a very simple but effective love spell. It is begun by cutting a heart out of a piece of red velvet. The heart must be at least five inches wide. As soon as the heart is ready, it is pierced with three new pins, while stating mentally that in the same manner will the lover's heart be pierced with love for the one casting the spell. Three pinches of dragon's blood are sprinkled over the heart, which is then burned inside a small cauldron. The cauldron must be filled with a very hot fire where three bay leaves have been dropped.

This spell is done to ensure the return of a lover or spouse who has abandoned the Witch for another person. It is important to mention the name of the rival and ask for the immediate return of the loved one.

Philters and Aphrodisiacal Foods

Philters and aphrodisiacal foods are very popular in Wicca and used by many Witches. Cumin is one of the most popular ingredients in this type of magic. Many Witches believe that a pinch of cumin in a glass of wine is infallible to conquer the love of a person. To ensure that the cumin is not detected, it can be introduced in the bottle of wine. Later a glass of the wine is offered to the person who will not notice anything amiss.

Something that is not very hygienic or recommended is also very popular in love magic. This consists of rubbing a piece of meat over the body after it has sweated freely and then cooking it and serving it to the person desired.

The Ritual of Desire

The Ritual of Desire is very popular in Wicca and is used by many Witches. As usual, the circle is cast first with the athame or the ficca.

The person must have bathed and purified himself ritually beforehand. The Lords of the Watch Towers are invoked in the east, south, west, and north and asked for their protection. As Witches work their magic in the north, the person must face this cardinal point as he starts this ritual. The lights are turned off and a red candle is lit in the center of the room.

A small, white dish with a few drops of water is placed in front of the candle. Any gold object, like a gold wedding band, is placed on the dish. The wish is written on a piece of parchment paper and held in the left hand. A handful of salt is taken with the right hand as the paper is placed over the gold object. As the wish is expressed aloud, the salt is allowed to fall slowly over the paper. The paper is picked up again with the left hand and burned in the candle's flame. When it is completely consumed, the gold object is removed and the ashes with the salt and the water are set aside to bury in the ground later. The candle is allowed to burn itself completely. The Lords of the Watch Towers are thanked and dismissed and the circle is vanished. This simple ritual may be utilized to acquire anything the Witch may desire. In healing cases, the candle should be yellow.

To Bind Love or Money

Many Witches tie candles when they want to achieve a special goal. A popular love spell is made by rubbing a red candle with musk oil, which is prepared beforehand by boiling mineral or jojoba oil with a handful of musk.

Before the candle is anointed, it is inscribed lengthwise with the name of the loved one. After the anointing, the candle is tied around the middle with a red ribbon and lit, while visualizing that the person's love has already been obtained by the one casting the spell. The candle is allowed to burn until it reaches the ribbon and is extinguished without blowing on it. The next day the spell is repeated with another candle and a new ribbon. This action is continued during seven days. The remnants of the candles and the ribbons are later buried near the loved one's home or in a place he or she frequents often.

The same spell may be used to obtain money but the candle and the ribbon must be green. The oil used to anoint the candle is bay leaf oil, prepared by boiling bay leaves in mineral oil. After the seventh day, the remnants of the candles and the ribbons are buried near the person's bank or a bank nearby.

A Money Bath

The money bath is very effective in the acquisition of money. A silver coin is placed in each of the compartments of an ice tray. The tray is filled with water and placed in the freezer. When the water in the tray has turned to ice, the bathtub is filled with very hot water and a few drops of bay leaf oil are added to the liquid. The ice cubes with the coins are thrown into the water and the person enters the bath. As the ice cubes melt in the hot water, the person visualizes large amounts of money coming into his or her possession. The person remains in the bath until the water has cooled. The coins are then picked up and spent as soon as possible so that the spell may take effect immediately.

A Power Amulet

Witches always carry amulets and talismans on their persons for power and protection. One of the most powerful amulets used in Wicca is prepared by securing a small leather pouch and filling it with the following stones: a jade, a tiger's eye, a Herkimer diamond, and a meteorite. Other ingredients added to the pouch are a shark's tooth, a magnet, and mandrake root. This amulet gives control over other persons and over every circumstance.

To energize the amulet, the Witch stands on top of a hill or a similar high place and faces east. This is done at sunrise during the waxing moon.

He raises the pouch between his hands and offers it to the rising sun, saying;

> *Aten, ruler of the firmament,*
> *By whose power man lives and dies.*
> *Eye of the sky, Radiant Sun,*
> *Let your will and mine be done.*
> *You and I are one.*
> *Charge this amulet with your power and strength.*

After this invocation, the Witch waits for a cosmic sign that his petition has been granted. This may come in the form of a sudden breeze, a bird's song, the tolling of a bell, or any sound or signal that may be interpreted favorably. When the sign has been received, he hangs the leather pouch around his neck with a leather strip. If the sign is not received, the petition has been denied and the ritual is null and the pouch must be undone.

The Witch carries the pouch on his person during seven days, removing it only before bathing or sleeping. After this time, the pouch is charged with the Witch's personal energies and must not be touched by anyone else.

The pouch may then be carried in a pocket or a handbag. When the Witch desires something, he writes the wish on a piece of parchment paper and places it in the pouch for seven days. Then he removes it and burns it in the flame of a red candle. Whatever he has wished for will be granted swiftly. This amulet also protects against sorceries and curses.

To Repel Sorceries and Curses

When a Witch wants to ensure that the evil wishes of an enemy will not harm him, he not only carries the Amulet of Power but also does a special ritual to repel sorceries and curses.

He begins by casting the circle with the athame in his usual place of work. He then lights a red candle and places a lit charcoal on his censer, adding frankincense, myrrh, and hyssop. He places three pinches of salt on the pentacle and fills the magic chalice with water, which he sets on the altar. With the tip of the athame he touches the salt which represents the Earth element. He then dips the tip of the athame in the water (Water element), and passes it through the candle flame (Fire element) and through the smoke of the incense (Air element). He repeats these actions three times and says:

> *Sacred elements protect me,*
> *From my enemy defend me,*
> *Earth and Water, Fire and Air.*
> *Let my enemy beware!*

With the tip of the athame he traces three circles around himself. The first circle is traced over his head; the second around his chest; and the third over the ground upon which he stands. He then spits three times into the censer and says:

> *All your sorceries and curses in this moment I undo.*
> *Any evil you may wish me will be returned unto you.*
> *In triple form they will bind you and they will be sent by me.*
> *By the power of the Goddess and the mighty Law of Three.*

After he says these words, the Witch stamps his foot on the ground three times. It is not necessary to name the enemy because the conjuring power is automatically directed to whoever did the sorcery or curse.

To Achieve Success in Business

The ingredients used in this amulet are a magnet stone, a lace agate, an aventurine, a labradorite, and a bit of spider's web. The web must be gathered after the spider has left it. The spider web is part of the spell because the spider is a symbol of work. The Witch cuts a piece of parchment paper in the shape of a circle and draws his zodiac sign upon it in green ink. He places the stones and the spider's web in the middle of the paper and ties it with a green ribbon. He passes the bundle through the smoke of frankincense, myrrh, and bay leaf and hides it in the place where he is employed, making sure that no one will find it.

The Power of Nature

Witches maintain a subtle but unbreakable bond with the forces of nature. Their homes are always filled with plants, birds, and other domestic animals. This connection with nature is so powerful that they can alter the weather, bring on the wind or vanish it, and attract or drive away storms. A Witch with well-developed powers can stop the rain, attract thunder and lightning, influence the tides, and determine the future by observing the flying patterns of birds and the actions of other animals.

The great power of trees is continuously being used by Witches. For example, gathering three small stones from the roots of a large tree and carrying them on the body or in a sachet bag gives power and good health. It is necessary to ask the tree's permission before picking up the stones and to thank it mentally for them. Hugging a tree and asking it for a bit of its great strength can help heal many illnesses, aches, and pains, especially migraines. When a Witch feels tired or weak, and in need of energy, he presses his forehead against the trunk of a strong tree and asks for its blessing, embracing the tree with love. He remains in this position for several minutes until he feels he has been revitalized. The reader may also try this any time he or she may wish to confirm its efficacy.

Nature responds to our love and it is not necessary to be a Witch to establish a strong link with its forces. It is sufficient to keep the parks and the rivers clean, to feed the birds and other wild animals, and to greet the wind, the sun, the moon, and the sea when one visits the beach.

Going out into the open air on a sunny day, opening one's arms and breathing deeply, while thanking nature for its bounties, is one of the simplest exercises, and one that nourishes the mind and the body with the purest and most powerful energies.

Petition to the Sea

There is a simple but very powerful ritual that is very popular with many Witches. It is used to ask the sea to grant a wish. The person removes his shoes and walks across the beach searching for something that belongs to the sea like a seashell, a stone, a piece of driftwood, a starfish, or seaweed. He picks up the object with his right hand or with the left if he is left-handed and visualizes strongly what he desires. He then walks towards the sea and stops at the tide line. He writes his wish on the sand with his index finger and throws the object into the water. He crosses his arms over his chest and says,

> *O great Mother, sea divine*
> *Everything was born from thee*
> *Bless me and all that is mine*
> *And let my wish come to me.*

He remains in this position until the waves rise to his feet and erase what he wrote on the sand. As soon as the words have disappeared, he thanks the sea and leaves the beach without looking backwards.

Star Power

Many people look up at the sky in the evenings and admire the beauty of the stars, but they are unaware of their great power. Witches know that every star that shines in the night sky is a sun or a planet that may be billions of light years away from us, but is ruled by cosmic forces of immense power. Each of those luminous points of light is charged with a great force, which may be used to ameliorate our human condition.

One of the ways the Witch works with star power is to identify with a particular star, which he chooses carefully. The moon should be waxing but not visible in the sky, as its light diminishes starlight.

The Witch observes the sky for a few moments until he sees a star that attracts him strongly. This then becomes his personal star. He carefully notes the star's position and, looking at it steadily, he says the following words:

Sidereal light, star of mine
That guides my life and my fate.
Show me always the right path
And may it always be straight.
May the One who marked your course
Let your light bring me good luck
In everything I desire
And wherever I may walk.

The Witch names his star, which he will always invoke whenever he is in trouble or has a special need. Sometimes the Witch uses a meteorite to establish a stronger link with his star. Because the meteorite is a celestial object that fell from the sky, it is believed to have a strong affinity with the stars. To establish the link between the meteorite and the star, the Witch takes the meteorite between his hands and lifts it towards the sky, saying:

Through your power and your light
Energize this meteorite.
May it be the link between us
Through the day and through the night.
I ask you this by the powers
of the Moon and of the Sun.
By the strength of my desire
In this night the spell is done.

After saying these words, the Witch places the meteorite inside a blue sachet bag, which he will always carry for help and protection. Whenever he desires to connect with his star's energy, he removes the meteorite from the bag, rubs it between his hands, and makes his petition.

The Anglo-Saxon Runes

In chapter 7 we discussed the Wicca Runes or Theban alphabet used by most modern Witches to inscribe their magical implements and to write to each other. Many Wiccan experts do not consider the Theban alphabet to be made of true Runes as Runes are usually formed by straight lines.

There are several types of Runes. Among them are the Runes used by the Scandinavian and Germanic peoples and by the Gauls, the Irish, the Scots, and all the Anglo-Saxons. The Druids, who were the priests of the ancient Celts, used a type of Rune known as Ogham. The ancient peoples did not use the Runes as an alphabet but as a divination system and also in magic rituals. Runes are very old and have great power.

Modern Witches use the Anglo-Saxon Runes in their magic work. These are based on the Germanic or Scandinavian Runes. The Theban alphabet, or Runes which we discussed earlier, is used by Wicca practitioners as a writing form, not for magical rituals or spells. The Runes used in the actual practice of magic are the Anglo-Saxon ones. In other words, there are two types of Runes: the Theban Runes, which are used for writing and to inscribe magical implements, and the Anglo-Saxon Runes, which are used in magic rituals.

The spoken Runes that are used during the ceremonies are not actually Runes but traditional invocations. Witches call them Runes perhaps as a symbol of the magic Runes they use in their rituals.

To the ancients the Runes represented concentrations of power. Each one was a symbol of an action or a human concern. They were used during divinations and to carry out powerful spells and rituals. In modern times they are still used as a divination tool that is very exact and effective. They are also used in magic rituals.

The Anglo-Saxon Runes are the ones used in divination and they may be easily obtained in New Age stores. They are composed of twenty-four designs engraved or drawn on different types of stones. The most common ones are engraved in terra cotta or clay. Others are inscribed in semiprecious stones like amethyst, hematite, moonstone, rose quartz, and others. The type of material on which they are engraved is not as important as the symbol and meaning of each Rune. In the next illustration you can see the various designs and their most basic meanings. In divination, Rune #25 is a blank Rune that represents destiny. (See the figures on the next page.)

There are several methods of Rune divination. In one of the simpler methods, the Runes are shaken inside the bag that contains them and one is then taken at random from the bag. This Rune predicts what is going to happen in the situation faced by the consultant. It is always important in the reading of the Runes, and in all forms of divination, to let intuition guide the person who is doing the interpretation. This is of great help in understanding the oracle.

Another form of reading the Runes is to remove four of the Runes from the bag and place them in a straight line facing the person who is reading them. The first Rune represents the past, the second symbolizes the present, the third represents the future, the fourth reveals the positive or negative influences surrounding the person.

The Anglo-Saxon Runes used in the practice of magic use only sixteen of the twenty-four traditional Runes.

Runes (Divination and Magic)

There are several forms to use the Runes in magic spells. Following is a list of several spells used by Witches that utilize the power of the Runes.

To Obtain a Person's Love

The Rune that symbolizes love is inscribed on an apple which is then given to the loved one. If the person eats the apple, the desired results are guaranteed.

Runes (Divination and Magic)

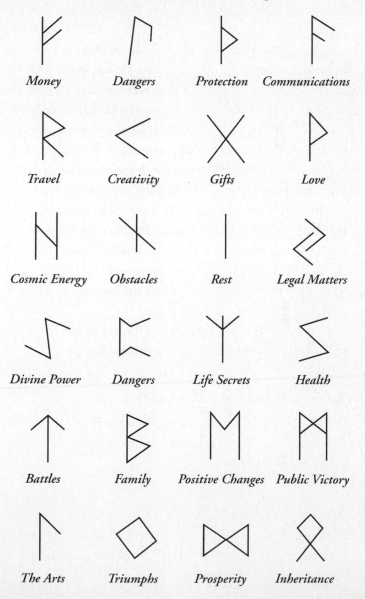

Money   Dangers   Protection   Communications

Travel   Creativity   Gifts   Love

Cosmic Energy   Obstacles   Rest   Legal Matters

Divine Power   Dangers   Life Secrets   Health

Battles   Family   Positive Changes   Public Victory

The Arts   Triumphs   Prosperity   Inheritance

To Heal a Person at a Distance

The Rune that symbolizes health is drawn on a piece of parchment paper. The name of the person who is ailing is written over the Rune. The paper is burned over the flame of a blue candle. The ashes are dispersed in the wind.

To Win a Court Case

The appropriate Rune is inscribed with a nail on a hematite. It is passed through an incense of bay leaf, myrrh, and storax. It is held in the hand during the trial.

To Win at Games of Chance

The Rune pertaining to games of chance is written on the money that will be used to play with money water. The money water is prepared by boiling bay leaf, chamomile flowers, cumin, and cinnamon in water. The Rune will be invisible, but its power will energize the bills.

To Obtain a Bank Loan

The Rune that symbolizes triumph is drawn with money water on the application papers and is passed through the smoke of a mixture of frankincense, myrrh, and cumin. The papers are then filled and submitted to the bank.

To Protect the Home

The Rune that represents the home is drawn on a piece of white cloth. A mixture of hyssop, spearmint, and sugar is placed in the middle of the cloth, which is tied with a white ribbon. The tied bundle is placed near the front door where no one will see or touch it.

To Conceive a Child

The fertility Rune is drawn on the woman's lower abdomen with fertility oil. The oil is prepared by boiling mistletoe, mandrake root, Adam and Eve roots, and vervain in mineral oil. This is repeated every night before sleep until she conceives.

To Obtain Money

The money Rune is drawn with blue ink on a bill of a high denomination. The corners of the bill are anointed with patchouli oil. The bill must be spent immediately, visualizing its return to the person multiplied by a thousand fold.

To Win a Battle

The war Rune is inscribed on a red candle and rubbed with bay leaf oil. It is then passed through the smoke of frankincense, myrrh, and olibanum. The candle is lit and allowed to consume itself visualizing that the battle has been won. The spell is repeated during seven consecutive nights at the stroke of midnight.

For Protection During a Trip

The Rune that represents a trip is drawn on a piece of parchment paper with yellow ink. The paper is placed inside an envelope with a feather. The name of the person is written on the envelope with a fictitious address at the city of the trip's destination.

For Good Luck in All Endeavors

The love Rune is drawn in red ink on a piece of parchment paper. Next to the love Rune is drawn the Rune of triumph with blue ink. This is followed by the money Rune in green ink. Lastly, the life Rune is drawn on the paper with violet ink.

The paper is passed through the smoke of frankincense, myrrh, and cinnamon and placed in a blue sachet bag with an agate, a rose quartz, a pyrite, and a lapis lazuli. Each stone represents one of the Runes. The sachet bag is carried in a pocket or the handbag.

Runes are used in many forms. Once the meaning of each Rune is known, it is possible to create many magic spells with them.

During this short treatise on Wicca, its rituals, its secrets, and its spells have been revealed to the Reader, who is invited to try some of these ancient magics for help and protection. As it was mentioned earlier, it is not necessary to be a Witch to use some of the ancient power and wisdom which is Wicca's legacy. But it is important to remember that all magic acts like a magnet and an echo. The spells and rituals found in this book should only be used for positive purposes. If they are used to harm another person, the one doing the adverse magic will soon be the recipient of the effects of the Law of Three. For that reason, it will be wise to bear in mind the Witch's rede:

An' it harm none,
Do as thou wilt.

EPILOGUE

My intention in writing this book has been, as in all my previous works, to instruct the Reader on the various magical systems. As I have explained in other books, magic is mental power used by an individual to effect positive changes in his or her life. This may be accomplished in many ways, including only the person's will power. But because not everyone has the power and the determination to reach his goals unaided, "magical" practices have been found to strengthen will power and direct it wisely. Because of their great beauty and antiquity, Wicca's beliefs and practices have been an intrinsic part of world magic. In modern times we can find Witch's covens in all parts of the planet, from Russia and Japan to New Zealand and Latin America. Because of their Celtic roots, inherited from Spain, Latin Americans have always been profoundly involved with magical practices, especially those of Wicca.

The word "Witchcraft" has always had a negative connotation for many people. But in reality, most Witches rarely employ their knowledge to harm other people or to control others. Witches embrace Wicca as their religion, not as a way to control their environment. Wicca is essentially a religion, as sacred and vital as other world religions. And like other religions, it has its deities, its myths, its beliefs, its rules and commandments, its priests, its holidays, its practices, and its faith. Its central foundation is nature and all of its laws. For that reason Witches protect all nature's creatures, who they consider their brethren. Witches maintain a constant identification with the flora, the fauna, the waters, the winds and all natural phenomena. A Witch's profound belief in the soul of nature allows him to establish a subtle contact with everything that exists and nature itself entrusts its most precious secrets to his care. For this reason a Witch may do "magic acts" that would seem impossible to people unfamiliar with Wicca. A highly developed Witch may stop or bring the rain, raise the wind or calm it, and carry out other magical actions equally astonishing. Because of his great sensitivity and spirituality, he recognizes the existence of invisible entities such as fairies, gnomes, undines, elves, salamanders, and many others, which exist on other dimensions or states of being. These creatures possess great powers because the various astral planes are the matrix of our physical world and everything that happens in the physical world must first be created on the higher planes.

Witches know this, and through their contacts with these astral beings may achieve extraordinary transformations in their daily lives. All of this is possible because of their faith in their own powers and the powers of nature.

Anyone can do the same if he remembers that everything is possible for those who believe.

The worst enemy of humanity is rank materialism. When a person only believes in what he can see and in the physical forms of the world that surround him, he becomes enslaved by matter. He loses the sublime contact with true reality which is the spirit, and becomes deaf and blind to the wonders that nature offers us continually. He cannot perceive the language of the animals and the plants. He does not know that stones sing and that waters have their own special intelligence. He does not know that trees and plants have an immense treasure that is at his disposal and that every leaf is a poem to the Creator of the Universe. This is a great tragedy. If all of humanity were determined to know and love nature, and sought God in the most humble creatures, we would have uncovered the secrets of the universe a long time ago, and we would live in peace and harmony. This is Wicca's lesson. If this book has helped you understand it, I will feel amply recompensed.

> *I put a spell on you*
> *Because you're mine.*
> *You better stop*
> *The things that you're doin'.*
> *I said, Watch out!*
> *I ain't lyin'.*
> *I ain't gonna take none of your*
> *Foolin' around.*

I ain't gonna take none of your
Puttin' me down.
I put a spell on you
Because you're mine.

—Screamin' Jay Hawkins

BIBLIOGRAPHY

Adler, M. *Drawing Down the Moon*. New York, 1980.

Buckland, R. *The Truth About Spirit Communication*. St. Paul, MN, 1996.

————. *Practical Candleburning Rituals*. St. Paul, MN, 1998.

————. *Wicca, Rituals and Practices of Witchcraft*. St. Paul, MN, 1999.

Cabot, L. and T. Cowan. *Power of the Witch*. New York, 1990.

Cunningham, S. *Living Wicca*. St. Paul, MN, 1982.

————. *The Truth About Witchcraft Today*. St. Paul, MN, 1987.

————. *Encyclopedia of Magical Herbs*. St. Paul, MN, 1985.

Farrar, S. *What Witches Do*. London, 1983.

Frost, G. and Y. Frost. *The Witch's Bible*. Los Angeles, 1976.

Gardner, G. *Witchcraft Today*. London, 1954.

González-Wippler, M. *The Complete Book of Spells, Magic, and Ceremonies*. St. Paul, MN, 1986.

———. *The Complete Book of Amulets and Talismans*. St. Paul, MN, 1990.

Grammary, A. *The Witch's Workbook*. New York, 1973.

Griggs, B. *The Green Witch Herbal*. London, 1993.

Huebner, L. *Power Through Witchcraft*. New York, 1971.

Kunz, G. F. *The Curious Lore of Precious Stones*. Canada, 1941.

Lady Sheba, *The Grimoire of Lady Sheba*. St. Paul, MN, 1972.

Leek, S. *Cast Your Own Spell*. New York, 1970.

———. *Diary of a Witch*. New York, 1968.

———. *The Complete Art of Witchcraft*. New York, 1971.

Martello, L. *Witchcraft: The Old Religion*. Secaucus, NJ, 1973.

Morrison, S. L. *The Modern Witch's Spellbook*. New York, 1987.

Sanders, A. *The Alex Sanders Lectures*. New York, 1980.

Silbey, U. *The Complete Crystal Guidebook*. New York, 1987.

Svensson, H. *The Runes*. New York, 1999.

Slater, H. *A Book of Pagan Rituals*. York Beach, ME, 1978.

Valiente, D. *Natural Magic*. London, 1975.

———. *An ABC of Witchcraft Past and Present*. New York, 1973.

Wedeck, H. E., ed. *Treasury of Witchcraft*. New York, 1961.

Worth, V. *The Crone's Book of Words*. St. Paul, MN, 1994.

Free Catalog

Get the latest
information on our
body, mind, and spirit products!
To receive a **free** copy of Llewellyn's consumer
catalog, *New Worlds of Mind & Spirit,* simply
call 1-877-NEW-WRLD or visit our website at
www.llewellyn.com and click on *New Worlds.*

LLEWELLYN ORDERING INFORMATION

Order Online:
Visit our website at www.llewellyn.com, select your books, and order
them on our secure server.

Order by Phone:
- Call toll-free within the U.S. at 1-877-NEW-WRLD
  (1-877-639-9753). Call toll-free within Canada at
  1-866-NEW-WRLD (1-866-639-9753)
- We accept VISA, MasterCard, and American Express

Order by Mail:
Send the full price of your order (MN residents add 6.5% sales tax) in
U.S. funds, plus postage & handling to:

> **Llewellyn Worldwide**
> **2143 Wooddale Drive, Dept. 978-0-7387-0213-1**
> **Woodbury, MN 55125-2989**

Postage & Handling:

> **Standard** (U.S., Mexico, & Canada). If your order is:
> > $24.99 and under, add $3.00
> > $25.00 and over, FREE STANDARD SHIPPING
>
> AK, HI, PR: $15.00 for one book plus $1.00 for
> each additional book.
>
> **International Orders** (airmail only):
> > $16.00 for one book plus $3.00 for each additional book

Orders are processed within 2 business days.
Please allow for normal shipping time. Postage and handling rates subject to change.